Writing a CV

Robert Leach

NATIONAL EXTENSION COLLEGE

BRITISH REFUGEE COUNCIL

Originated and devised by
Peter Knatchbull-Hugessen and Marie Needham

Written by Robert Leach

Commissioned by the British Refugee Council
240–250 Ferndale Road
London SW9 8BB

Tel. 0171 582 6922

Published by the National Extension College

© The National Extension College Trust Ltd. All rights reserved.

First edition 1989
Reprinted in 1993, 1995

ISBN 0 86082 939 1

No part of this publication may be reproduced, stored in a retrieval system, or transmitted in any form or by any means, electronic, mechanical, photocopying, recording, or otherwise, without prior permission of the publisher.

This publication is sold subject to the condition that it shall not by way of trade or otherwise, be lent, resold, hired out, or otherwise circulated without the publisher's prior consent in any form of binding or cover other than that in which it is published and without a similar condition being imposed on the subsequent purchaser.

The National Extension College is an educational trust and a registered charity with a distinguished body of trustees. It is an independent, self-financing organisation.

Since it was established in 1963, NEC has pioneered the development of flexible learning for adults. NEC is actively developing innovative materials and systems for distance learning opportunities on over 100 courses, from basic skills and general education to degree and professional training.

For further details of NEC resources and supported courses, contact:

National Extension College Trust
18 Brooklands Avenue
Cambridge CB2 2HN

Tel. 01223 316644; Fax. 01223 313586
Customer Services direct line 01223 358295

Printed in Great Britain by NEC Print
Typeset by Cambridge Photosetting Services
Designed by David Cutting Graphics, Cambridge

how to use this book

You can do it on your own
This is a self-study course. That means it is a book that functions as a teacher. It sets you tasks to do, and when you have done the tasks it often gives you answers or suggested answers. By doing the tasks you build up the skills you need to be able to write your own **CVs** and supporting statements.

Do it all
You should follow the instructions in the book and do all the tasks, otherwise you won't be ready to write your CV in the most effective way.

Keep going . . .
At the beginning of each unit is a suggestion of the period of time needed to complete the unit. Before you start a unit, make sure that you have got enough free time to complete it quickly, within a day or a few days. You should also plan regular study and writing time so that you can complete the whole course in a reasonably short stretch of time – perhaps six weeks.

. . . until you get a job
Although this is a self-study course, that doesn't mean that you should keep it a secret. It is very important to show your work to other people for their comments and to involve them in helping you. If you are on a course or training scheme, your tutor or instructor will help you, but you still need to find other people who are able and willing to work with you to make your CV as good as it can possibly be. By doing this, you have a better chance of getting a useful and rewarding job.

contents

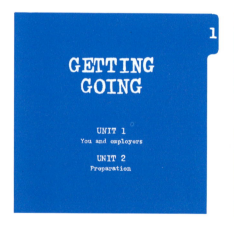

GETTING GOING 1

UNIT 1
You and employers

UNIT 2
Preparation

page 7

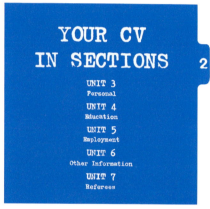

YOUR CV IN SECTIONS 2

UNIT 3
Personal

UNIT 4
Education

UNIT 5
Employment

UNIT 6
Other Information

UNIT 7
Referees

page 25

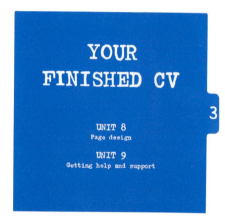

YOUR FINISHED CV 3

UNIT 8
Page design

UNIT 9
Getting help and support

page 65

page 75

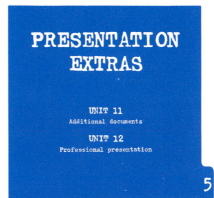

page 85

Acknowledgements

London Borough of Camden Application Form
King's College Hospital Internal Advertisement
National Extension College/Basic Skills Unit PIC
NARIC, British Council, Spring Gardens, SW1

GETTING GOING

UNIT 1
You and employers

UNIT 2
Preparation

UNIT 1   YOU AND EMPLOYERS

Introduction
Positive attitudes
Employer expectations

TASK 1   **List questions employers may have**
TASK 2   **How to deal with questions**
TASK 3   **Answer special questions**

The seven point plan: physical condition, attainments, intelligence, aptitudes, interests, disposition, circumstances.

TASK 4   **Use a CV to answer questions in the plan**

The employer's point of view.

TASK 5   **Describe yourself in terms of the seven point plan**

UNIT 2   PREPARATION

CVs compared with Application Forms. Standard Graduate application form. Strategies for dealing with application forms.

TASK 6   **Make form work as a CV**

Equal Opportunity employers. Camden equal opportunity form.

TASK 7   **Answer equal opportunity questions**

CV's and Personal Information Charts.

TASK 8   **Make a PIC style CV**

Cultural problems. Angel Nogales, Paul Burnett, Janet Herriot CVs.

TASK 9   **Compare US and UK CVs**

Checking your English

TASK 10   **Evaluate different approaches to correct English**

Planning the order

TASK 11   **Plan order of elements in CV**

Application letters

you and employers

This first unit helps you to understand the employer's point of view. It is much easier to write a CV if you know what the employer is looking for. You will also think about how your CV can present the information the employer needs to make a decision about you.

Time needed for this unit: 2 hours

WHY A CV?

Question: Why write a CV? Answer: It helps you to get a job.

The information you give in a CV interests the employer in your **skills** and personality. **The way you handle the CV shows the employer how you may handle a job.** If your CV gives only information that is relevant, it shows that you will probably not waste time in the job. If the CV is well-organised and looks good, it suggests you are well-organised and you will present yourself well to colleagues and customers.

CVs are needed for most professional jobs. Your CV is used by the employer to see if you can do a professional job in presenting information about yourself. If you can write a CV well, you are probably good at other things too!

Three-quarters of British jobs are filled without advertising. Even if you don't see advertisements for the job you want, and you don't have personal contacts, you can still send your CV to likely employers. If it's the right CV for a current vacancy, it can be almost as good as a personal contact.

Writing a CV is a skill, and can be learned like any other skill. You don't need perfect English or detailed knowledge of British culture but you do need to spend a lot of time and effort preparing a good CV.

CV = *Curriculum vitae* (Latin). A summary of your past education, employment, personal details and skills, which will help you find employment. Also known as **career history, personal information, personal details, personal background** and various other terms.

How does this course help you do that?

units 1 & 2	The **getting going** part helps to prepare you by looking at what employers expect from job applicants.
units 3, 4, 5, 6 & 7	The **CV in sections** part takes you through the CV step by step.
units 8 & 9	The **finished CV** part helps you to present the CV well and avoid errors.
unit 10	The **supporting statement** part gives ideas for writing a positive explanation to go with your CV, as many employers require this. The same ideas can be used for writing an application letter for any job.
units 11 & 12	Finally the **presentation extras** part deals with other documents that you should have ready for job applications, and how to give your CV a professional appearance.

BE POSITIVE

You have a range of experience which may be unfamiliar to employers, but which could be very useful to them. Many of the most successful people in Britain, ranging from millionaire businessmen to Nobel prize-winning scientists, started in this country as refugees. Don't imagine that you lack employable skills or that employers are too prejudiced and ignorant to look at them. If you show that you are willing and able, most employers will consider you seriously.

WHAT WILL EMPLOYERS WANT TO KNOW ABOUT REFUGEES?

Before we look at what employers expect of a job applicant, let's think about some special questions they'll have in mind about you as a refugee.
- How good is your English?
- Does your work permit have any special conditions?
- How relevant is your foreign employment experience?
- What level are your qualifications?
- Do you intend to return to your home country?

TASK 1

Can you think of any other special questions that may be in an employer's mind to ask a refugee? Write your ideas on a separate piece of paper. Then look under Task 1 Answers at the end of this unit for my suggestions.

Now let's think about how you can answer these questions. **It's important to realise that indirect answers are often more effective than direct ones.** For instance, it is best to show how well you speak and write English by writing a good CV and performing well at an interview, rather than by saying "my English is very good."

TASK 2

Here is something that a refugee said at an interview. Which of the employer's questions above are being answered?

> 'The political situation in my country is very bad, and will be bad for some time. It is no place for a social democrat like me. Fortunately my children are doing very well at school here, and we feel safe. The Architects Registration Council is being helpful. Have you seen these photos of some of my buildings?'

Look at the answers at the end of the unit.

TASK 3

Look back to Task 1 where you suggested some special questions an employer might have. How could you answer these questions indirectly either in a CV or in an interview? Some suggested answers are at the end of this unit.

WHAT DO EMPLOYERS LOOK FOR?

Employers often use a **seven point plan**. This is a checklist of the questions that employers need answers to about any job applicant. This list, or something like it, is used during interviews and afterwards to choose which applicant should get the job. Although employers consider these points at interview stage, your CV can help to answer many of them in a positive way. This will persuade an employer to give you an interview in the first place. It will also create a good impression before the interview actually takes place.

TASK 4

Look at the points in the seven point plan below. Which ones can you answer in your CV? Make a note of where or how you could answer them in your CV. Then look at the suggestions at the end of this unit.

The Seven-Point Plan

1 **Physical make-up** — health, appearance, bearing and speech.
2 **Attainments** — education, qualifications, experience.
3 **General intelligence** — intellectual capacity.
4 **Special aptitudes** — mechanical, manual dexterity, facility in use of words and figures.
5 **Interests** — intellectual, practical, constructional, physically active, social, artistic.
6 **Disposition** — acceptability, influence over others, steadiness, dependability, self-reliance.
7 **Circumstances** — any special demands of the job, such as ability to work unsocial hours, travel abroad, etc.

HOW WOULD AN EMPLOYER SEE YOU?

Now that you have thought about the seven point plan, try to look at it from the point of view of an employer. That will help you to write your CV in a way that will satisfy the employer on all seven points.

TASK 5

Below is an employer's **interview record**, using the seven point plan. What information would you put about yourself in this record? Fill it in as you would like an employer to fill it in about you. In this situation, you can be a little more boastful than usual! After all, your potential employers probably want to write good things about you if they have gone to the trouble of interviewing you.

```
                    INTERVIEW RECORD

    Name:                           Date:
    Post:
    Name of Interviewer(s):
    _____

    Assessment of Candidate:

    1.  Appearance and Physique:


    2.  Educational and/or Vocational Attainments:
        (Comment on standard reached)


    3.  General Intelligence / Common Sense:


    4.  Special Aptitudes:


    5.  Interests:


    6.  Personality / Disposition / Ambition:


    7.  Circumstances (e.g. mobility; proximity to work; availability of hours):
```

Interview record = a form the employer fills in to note the important qualities and experience of a person being interviewed for a job.

That is the end of the first unit.
You have learned to understand the employer's point of view, and have used the seven point plan to work out how you will put across the relevant information in a CV.

ANSWERS

Other possible questions are: Will this person be able to make good working relationships with British staff? Is his/her general knowledge of the UK good enough?	**TASK 1**
It answers questions 5 and 3. His general level of English also answers question 1.	**TASK 2**

ANSWERS continued

TASK 3 The questions I suggested for Task 1 could be answered by general friendly behaviour and by showing knowledge of British institutions (e.g. school, Architects Registration Council). You will have different answers.

TASK 4 1. Physical condition. You can describe your physical condition in the "Personal" section of your CV. This is covered in Unit 3.

2. Attainments. Questions about attainments can be answered in the CV by listing your educational and career achievements. Units 4 and 5 cover these.

3. General intelligence. Your use of only relevant information in your CV, and a clear presentation, shows your intelligence.

4. Special aptitudes. Include aptitudes in the "Other information" section(s) of your CV. This is covered in Unit 6.

5. Interests. Only include a few interests in your CV, preferably those which directly relate to the job, but be ready to talk about your other interests at interviews. Unit 6 covers this.

Assessment = judgement based on tests

6. Disposition. The CV can prepare the ground for a good **assessment** of your disposition at interview. **It should show confidence in your strengths but not over-confidence.** Compare these three examples of statements about employment. One is too boastful, one is too humble, and one is about right. Which is which?

a. I ran the best shoe shop in the country; fantastic profits every year and great write-ups in the newspapers.

b. I was only a simple shoe seller.

c. I owned and managed a successful shoe retailing business with a national reputation. Press clippings available.

(a. boastful   b. too humble   c. about right)

7. Circumstances. There are advantages and disadvantages in explaining your circumstances fully at CV stage. See Unit 3, *Personal,* for more details.

preparation

unit 2

In Unit 2 you will do some general planning for your CV. We will be comparing it with an application form, looking at cultural and English language issues, and deciding on the headings and order of the information in your CV.

Time needed for this unit: 2 hours

CVS COMPARED WITH APPLICATION FORMS

A CV and an application form both give the employer information about you. **The difference is that the employer designed the application form, and you design your CV.**

Your CV and your application form may give two very different pictures of your life. Many **careers advisers** think that for professional or executive jobs you should send your CV along with any completed application form, unless the employer specifically instructs you not to send a CV. If you send both a form and a CV, the employer can look at your background in two different ways.

In a job application form, you have to decide what to put in, what to leave out and how to present all the information. The form is always designed for British people with British educational, employment and personal backgrounds. There is often not enough space for some items, and there are usually headings where it is difficult to put anything in at all.

If you have trouble filling in an application form because it has the wrong headings or not enough space, you can add an extra sheet of paper with the relevant information. You can also change the headings to suit your experience. This will be in your favour if it is done in a way that shows the employer more about your suitability for the job. You can also attach a CV to your form, as suggested above.

Now let's look at what you have to do to write a CV. Unlike an application form, a CV is entirely up to you. You design it as well as write it. That fact is very helpful. You can choose the headings, and the length (up to two pages), and you can design it to make your life look

Headings = words at the top of a section of writing to show the subject or topic of it.

as good as it possibly can.

It is important to rethink and, often, rewrite your CV for every new job application. Different jobs require you to stress different aspects of your life.

To help your first design for your CV, let's look at an application form. Application forms vary a lot. Here is the standard Graduate Careers Advisory Service application form, as used in all British universities and polytechnics. It may not be suitable for you. It is meant for new graduates so it probably contains many headings that you don't need, and leaves out others that you do need. That doesn't matter – it is just a useful starting point.

Form (page 2)

Describe any aspect of your course of particular interest to you and/or of relevance to your application

Any other qualifications/skills, eg knowledge of foreign languages (indicate proficiency), keyboard skills, computer literacy.

Current driving licence? Yes / No

Activities and Interests
Give details of your main extra curricular activities and interests to date. What have you contributed and what have you got out of them? Mention any posts of responsibility

Work Experience
Name of employer	From	To	Type of work, including sandwich placements, vacation and part-time work. Include voluntary work.

Which parts of this experience were most beneficial to you, and why?

Form (page 3)

Career choice
Explain what attracts you about the type(s) of work for which you are applying and offer evidence of your suitability

Please mention any points you wish to raise at interview

Do you have any restrictions on geographical mobility and/or a strong preference for a particular location? If so, give details

If you feel there is anything which has not been covered adequately elsewhere on your application, please elaborate below

Have you any family connection or other contact with this organization? If so give details

Health matters of possible relevance - colour blindness, etc

Dates not available for interview | Date available for employment

Referees, one of whom should be academic. Give name, address and occupation (BLOCK LETTERS)

1. Postcode / Telephone
2. Postcode / Telephone

Date | Signature

TASK 6

Look at the form and delete any headings that you would not use to apply for your preferred kind of job. Add any other headings that you would use.

Does this list of headings look right for your CV? Write them down, and consult them as you work through the different parts that make up your CV in this course.

Applicants and **candidates** = people who apply for a job.

Local authorities = the government of a small part of the UK, such as Birmingham, Surrey, Brighton or Camden.

Equal opportunities = against unfair treatment of women, ethnic minorities, poorer and disabled people.

EQUAL OPPORTUNITY EMPLOYERS

Most executive job **applicants** are white, middle-class, British males. But many **local authorities** and social organisations do try to be fair and make jobs equally open to women, black people and other ethnic minorities and disabled **candidates** by a special selection process. This process involves giving each candidate points for every way that their experience matches the job requirements. So, for these jobs it is all the more important to make sure that your CV is exactly tailored to the job's requirements.

Equal opportunity employers also like to check that they are recruiting people from disadvantaged groups, and so they ask for ethnic information on their application forms. A few jobs, requiring certain qualities, are allowed, by law, to favour women or people from a particular ethnic background. So you have a much greater chance of getting these jobs if you are a woman or from an ethnic minority.

Here is part of an equal opportunity employer's application form.

Section B

In order to ensure the Council's continued development of its declared equal opportunities policy (see adjacent column) all applicants for employment with Camden are asked to place a tick in the appropriate box below and complete the detail required. This information which will be used solely for monitoring purposes, will be treated as confidential and will be separated on receipt and before consideration of candidates takes place.

LONDON BOROUGH OF CAMDEN

Application for the post of ....

Vacancy Reference Number ....

1. I would describe my cultural and ethnic origin as: (indicate by placing an X in appropriate box)

African	_____	Chinese	_____
Asian	_____	Cypriot	_____
Caribbean	_____	Irish	_____
UK European	_____	Other European	_____

Any other (please specify) ....

2. My sex is (delete as appropriate) Male/Female

3. Name ....

First name(s) ....

Signed ....

Date: ....

TASK 7

Fill in your ethnic details on the form above. Then decide how you could include the same information in a CV addressed to an equal opportunity employer. Then check with the Answers section at the end of this unit.

EQUAL OPPORTUNITIES IN EMPLOYMENT

Introduction
The purpose of this statement is to make a clear commitment to the principle of Equal Opportunities and to outline ways in which the Council will implement its policy.

How the policy will work
The policy covers job applicants and all existing employees and is aimed particularly at helping groups of people who have special difficulty in getting a job or in gaining promotion, e.g. ethnic minorities, women and disabled persons.

Ethnic minority groups
This Council believes that it is in the interests of racial harmony, social justice and a more effective service to the community, to provide equal opportunities and fair treatment for all its employees regardless of race and colour.

Registered Disabled
The Council has a legal responsibility to employ a number of registered disabled people equal to 3% of its work force. There are special schemes for finding appropriate work and for the re-location of existing staff if they become disabled at work.

Women
This Council has taken and will continue to take positive steps to enable women to take advantage of increased career opportunities.

This Council has agreed, for example, a generous scheme for extended maternity leave, giving up to 40 weeks paid leave. There is also a staff day nursery.

Monitoring
The policy, to be effective, must be monitored (see Section B of the application form). This will help show what changes have taken place since the policy was introduced.

Grievance
A procedure has been introduced to deal with complaints relating to appointments (see on reverse).

Individual rights
No aspect of the Council's policy detracts in any way from a person's right to refer a case to an Industrial Tribunal or any other body which deals with the enforcement of the Sex Discrimination Act 1976 and Race Relations Act 1976.

PERSONAL INFORMATION CHART

Name: Age:

Address:

Date of birth:

Telephone No.

Education and training history:

Employment experience:

Special skills/interests:

References:

CVS AND PERSONAL INFORMATION CHARTS

The term "CV" is mainly used for jobs for office workers, not for manual jobs or jobs for young people. Other descriptions like "Personal History", or "Personal Details" or "Personal Information" are often used. Capital Radio and National Extension College developed a "Personal Information Chart (PIC)" for young people and it is now widely used.

Look at the PIC. Which headings would you use to apply for a non-office job? Add any other headings that you would use, and delete any that you wouldn't use. Check your ideas against the Answers section at the end of the Unit.

Does your list of headings now look ready for use in your PIC-style CV? Write them down and consult them as you work through the different parts of your CV in this course. Then you can have it ready for applying for suitable jobs.

TASK 8

CULTURAL PROBLEMS

As you know, your home country and Britain are culturally very different. You must be aware of cultural differences when you write a CV.

To give an example of how cultural differences can cause trouble, here is an American CV which you can compare with two British CVs from similar young graduates. See if you can tell the differences between the US and British approaches. This will help you guard against cultural problems yourself.

TASK 9

Compare Angel Nogales' CV with those of Paul Burnett, and Janet Herriot. What differences can you find? Check with the Answers section.

Personal Data Sheet

Angel Nogales
999 Carson Drive
Sacramento, CA 95804

(916) 351-7584

Date of Birth:	March 17, 1957
Place of Birth:	New York City
Citizenship:	United States
Height:	5 feet 8 inches
Weight:	135 pounds
Health:	Excellent

EDUCATION

Institution	Dates	Diploma Degree
Central High School Buffalo, BY 14213	1970–74	Commercial
Castleton Junior College Castleton, CA 95807 1974–76		A.A.S.

Major: Accounting   Scholastic Standing: 3.2 (B+)

Major Courses	Background Courses
Elementary and Advanced Accounting I, II, III, IV	Business Communications
Auditing	Business Law I, II
Income Tax Procedures	Money and Banking
Cost Accounting	Economic Analysis
Business Management	Marketing

EXTRACURRICULAR ACTIVITIES AND HONORS

Accounting Club, President (elected office) 1975–76
College Glee Club 1975–76
Phi Beta Lambda 1976 (honorary undergraduate business education association)
Future Business Leaders of America 1973–74
High-school valedictorian 1974

EXPERIENCE

Company	Dates	Job Duties
Hewlett-Packard Avionics 2072 Glen Valley Sacramento, CA 95804	April 1979 – present	Assistant Manager, Finance Office
	August 1976 – April 1979	Trainee Manager & Accounts Clerk, Finance Office.
Bullock's Department Store Sacramento, CA 95804	September 1974 to August 1976 (part-time)	Retail selling, Furnishings
Lane's	Summers 1973–1974	Stock clerk

REFERENCES

Dr James Kornbluth, Vice-President for Human Resources, Hewlett-Packard Avionics, 2072 Glen Valley, Sacramento, CA 95804.

Mr Frank Naber, Department Manager, Furnishings, Bullock's Department Store, 18 State Street, Sacramento, CA 95804.

Mrs Hazel Hines, 184 West School Street, Sacramento, CA 95602.

```
                    CURRICULUM VITAE                              CURRICULUM VITAE
                       Paul Burnett
                                                       NAME:            Janet Herriot
Date of Birth:   11th September 1963   Nationality: British
                                                       SEX:             Female              DOB: 2 April 1956
Address:        14 Briar Cottages, Dalestown, DT1 1XZ
                Tel: 0914 3209                         NATIONALITY:     British
                                                       HOME ADDRESS:    6, The Rocks, Kedleston, Derbyshire
                       EDUCATION
                                                       TELEPHONE:       0732 614611
1980–1981      Institute of Linguists Interpreting Course
               (French-English), Sunderland Polytechnic, Sunderland.
                                                       EDUCATION
1981           Interpreting Diploma (French-English), with
               Business French (Distinction).          1968–1974        Highgate Comprehensive School, Rugby

1973–1977      University of North Yorkshire, Huddle, North   Summer 1972   GCE 'O' Levels: Biology (A), English Language
               Yorkshire.                                                   (C), French (D), Mathematics (B), Physics (C),
                                                                            German (C).
1977           BA Hons. 2.2 Modern Languages (French, German).
                                                       Summer 1974      GCE 'A' Levels: Biology (B), Chemistry (C),
1968–1973      Moorland Comprehensive School, Ling Road, Dalestown.        Mathematics (C). School prize for Biology.
               GCE 'A' Levels (French (A), Latin (C), English (C));
               GCE 'O' Levels (French (B), Biology (D),   1974–1977      University of Warwick, B.Sc. Hons. 2.1.
               German (C), Maths (C), History (C), Latin (B).              Biology (specialising in entomology and ecology)

                     WORK EXPERIENCE                   WORK EXPERIENCE

1985–now       Interpreter (French-English), EEC Agricultural   1978–1982   Research Officer, Thames Water Authority,
               Commission, Boulevard Strauss, Strasbourg, France           Didcot, Berks.
               and EEC, Commission Centre, Brussels, Belgium.
                                                       1982–1985        Parenting and Household Management.
1981–1985      Interpreter and Translator, Thompson-Brandt SA,
               77 Boulevard Hausmann, 75017 Paris, France.   1985–1988    Part-time Lecturer in Biology ('A' Level),
                                                                         Derby College of Higher Education.
1977–1979      Interpreter and Technical Translator, Agro Mech
               Industriel SA, Toulon, France.          1988-present     Senior Researcher (Ecology), Trent Water
                                                                        Authority, Trafford.
                       INTERESTS
                                                       SKILLS           Good technical French and German (reading).
Member of International Ramblers Club. Participated in 4 Archaeological  Programming in Pascal, C, and Fortran-B.
digs (England, Turkey and Spain).
                                                       REFEREES

                       REFEREES                        H.A.L. Willoughby, FRS, D.Phil, B.Sc.
                                                       Trent Water Authority Research Laboratories
Herr Claus Richter            M. E.M. Fouquet, Director   Trafford, Lancashire
Head of Interpreting Unit     Service des Interpretes  TB3 107
EEC Agricultural Commission   Thompson-Brandt SA
Commission Centre             77 Boulevard Hausmann    Dr A.D. Davies, Director
Brussels, Belgium             75017 Paris, France      Thames Water Research
                                                       Didcot, Berkshire
                                                       BK2 4HO
```

Small details can make a big difference to employers' ideas about a person. Make sure that a British person understands your CV.

CHECKING YOUR ENGLISH

Good English is important in job applications, though it's often much less important once you get a job. Most English people think they have bad spelling and admit to problems with grammar, but it's much harder if English is not your first language. Your CV should look perfect, but your English probably isn't. How can you deal with this situation? Look at Task 10 to clarify your ideas.

TASK 10

Think about this situation. You have good spoken English, but your writing is not very good. You want to apply for a job that doesn't need much writing, but does need a CV. How would you go about it? Which of the suggestions listed below is nearest to what you would do? Why? If you have a different plan, put it in at Number 8. Then check with the Answers section.

1. Write the CV alone, and hope mistakes won't matter.

2. Write the CV alone, but carefully use the dictionary and a grammar book.

3. Write the CV alone, but include a note to explain about your good spoken English.

4. Write the CV with the help of a friend or self-help group.

5. Ask an English teacher or an Employment consultant to write the CV for you.

6. If you get an interview, tell the employer about your bad spelling and shaky grammar.

7. Make contact by phone and avoid using the CV at all.

8. ....

Now think about your own level of spoken and written English. Are you confident about it? If not, how can you improve it? If your writing is weak, you could consider following a self-study course. See the booklist on page 93.

Whatever you feel about your English, keep working through this book, and keep applying for jobs. Choose a way to cope with language problems, and remember that relatively few people have really good English.

PLANNING THE ORDER

As we saw in the case of Angel Nogales, the American CV has dates in the middle. In Britain, dates should be on the left or possibly right. Some CVs put personal information, like address and phone number, somewhere in the middle of the page. This is a mistake as it makes your address or number difficult to find when an employer wants to contact you. The usual order of sections is: Personal, Education, Employment, Other Information section(s), and finally, Referees. We will follow that order here, but many people (particularly those with good past jobs) put Employment after Personal and before Education. In the Employment section you should normally put your last job first, and then go backwards through time to your first job. This is called **reverse chronological order**. You can choose to go forwards instead if your recent jobs were not very good ones.

Plan the order of your CV:	
Dates left or right?	left/right
Employment before or after Education?	before/after
Reverse chronological order or not?	reverse/not

TASK 11

APPLICATION LETTERS

It is best to think about application letters when you have gone through the stages of writing a CV and a **supporting statement**. An application letter can be a short letter attached to your CV, or it can occasionally be a long letter rather like a CV. If an advertisement says "please apply by letter stating your experience and reasons for suitability", they expect a long letter like an essay. You can use your CV as your notes for it. However these long letters are very unusual. To write a normal, short application letter, write your CV first. Pick out two or three good points from it that are relevant to the job, and put them in the letter. See Unit 10, *Supporting statements*, for more details of how to choose the best items from your CV.

Supporting statement – see Unit 10.

In this unit you have planned the headings for your CV, comparing it with an application form. You have added ethnic details for use with equal opportunity employers. You have thought about issues of culture and English language level, and planned the order of the items in your CV. You are now ready to plan how to write your CV.

ANSWERS

Here is an example of how one refugee put her ethnic group on her CV:

Nationality: Ghanaian (no work permit required)
Ethnic group: Black (African)

TASK 7

ANSWERS continued

TASK 8 You should probably use all the headings in the PIC. See Unit 6 for ways to present the information listed as "Special Skills/Interests" on the PIC, and also extra headings which you could add to your PIC.

One other heading is not so often used for professional or office-based jobs, but it can be quite important. This heading is "Equipment I can use". In a technical job you need to know how to use the relevant equipment – machines, tools, instruments or other items. For example, a job as draughtsperson or draughtsman (technical drawing) may require use of Computer Aided Drafting/Design (CAD). So an applicant for this kind of job might write:

Equipment I can use

AutoCAD, PLUTO and PATRAN-G software on PS300, PDP-11 and CDC 7600 computers, using digitiser, tablet, lightpen and puck inputs.

Even if you do not think that the equipment you can use will be relevant in the job you want, you can show that your skills with one type of equipment are useful with another type. See Unit 5 for more details on showing how you can transfer your skills from one kind of job to another.

Does your list of headings now look ready for use in your PIC-style CV? Keep it with you and consult it as you work through the parts of your CV in this course. Then you can have it ready for applying for suitable jobs.

TASK 9 Angel calls her CV a "Personal Data Sheet". This would sound pretentious in the UK. The other US terms for a CV are "Résumé", "Qualifications sheet", "Biodata" and "Summary". They would sound odd in the UK.

Angel includes her height and weight (in pounds, not pounds and stones or kilos!) To a British employer this suggests too much concern about personal appearance.

There is no concept of "scholastic standing" in the UK, and the initials "A.A.S." are unknown.

Angel mentions "honors". Honours (British spelling) in Britain would normally mean awards given by the Queen to important citizens.

Angel puts the dates of her education and employment in the middle of the page. British employers would usually expect them on the left, or perhaps the right. To put them in the middle is less acceptable.

TASK 10 There are no sure answers, but it's certainly better to use a friend, self-help group, dictionary and grammar book than hope mistakes won't matter. Don't explain about good spoken English in a CV, show it in a phone call or interview.

YOUR CV IN SECTIONS

2

UNIT 3
Personal

UNIT 4
Education

UNIT 5
Employment

UNIT 6
Other Information

UNIT 7
Referees

UNIT 3 PERSONAL

The minimum personal information: name, address, date of birth

Names – Naming systems and presentation of names.

Date of birth. Problems of discrepancies.

Other personal information.

Telephone – Need for contact number. Strategies for language problems on phone.

Age. Courtesy inclusion.

Place of birth, nationality, NI number. Whether to make refugee status obvious.

Gender/sex. Marital status. Advantages of being single for women and married for men. Children. Need to include childcare arrangements. Nuclear family.

Health. Where to explain past health problems.

Review of headings. Shler Karim & Scott Naylor CVs.

TASK 12 **Choose which items to include from a checklist of personal information items**

MAIN TASK A **Complete "Personal" section of CV**

* = example answer given

UNIT 4 EDUCATION

Education and training. Dates, institution, course, qualification. Difference between training and education. Deciding what to put under "Education" and what under another section.

TASK 13 **Categorise courses under "Education" and "Other information".***

Matching your qualifications with British ones. Validation of qualifications (DES/British Council). NARIC.

TASK 14 **Apply to NARIC for equivalence assessment**

TASK 15 **Use reference book to compare British system and qualifications (general and professional, examples teaching and accountancy) with home country's**

Attitudes to overseas qualifications. Undervaluing. Advice (doors not closed) – WUS.

Language competence. English language competence and qualifications. Value of English language qualifications for various types of employment.

Sequence English language qualifications in order of acceptability to UK employers at particular status levels	TASK 16

Gaps in your education. Interrupted education and evidence needed. Ways to explain gaps. Brenda Hopkins CV.

Fill in "Educational" section of CV	MAIN TASK B

* = example answer given

EMPLOYMENT UNIT 5

Describing your past jobs.	TASK 17

Dates, job title, employer. Need to give short (5–20 word) descriptions. Inclusion of staff numbers supervised, but not reasons for leaving or salary. Jobs without British versions – examples noodlemaker, dramaturg.

Draft notes describing previous jobs in 5, 10 and 20 words	TASK 18

Critical review of job descriptions.

Analyse and improve sample job descriptions*	TASK 19

Technical translations. Sources of information – textbooks, agencies, dictionaries, CRCs, NEC bilingual dictionaries.

Write five technical terms from past jobs and find English equivalents	TASK 20

Addresses. Detail needed. Contact names and addresses or why they are absent. Need for evidence. What omissions usual. Level of detail.

List addresses and contact names of all past jobs	TASK 21

Gaps. Where and how to explain gaps in career – political reasons, unemployment, failed in businesses, childcare and household management. Health reasons in other section. Marian Burwood CV.

Choose suitable explanations for gaps in employment	TASK 22
Courses to show employers your skills	TASK 23
Find suitable local courses.	
Complete "Employment" section of CV	MAIN TASK C

* = example answer given

UNIT 6   OTHER INFORMATION

Possible headings. Interests, achievements, skills, hobbies, personal qualities, extra-curricular activities, publications, research, professional associations. Stress need to show skills not just hobbies.

TASK 24   **Choose relevant headings for a range of skills and achievements,* and then headings for own CV**

Explaining gaps.

Choosing the right items.

TASK 25   **Choose items for particular jobs***

MAIN TASK D   **Write "Other information" section(s) of CV**

* = example answer given

UNIT 7   REFEREES

Kinds of referee. Professional, educational and personal.

Professional referees.

Academic referees.

Personal referees.

TASK 26   **Choosing referees among several possibles***

Asking permission.

TASK 27   **Gap-fill letter to referee***

The reference itself.

MAIN TASK E   **Choose and get permission from three referees**

Fill in the "Referees" section of the CV

* = example answer given

personal

unit 3

In this unit we will go through the categories of personal information that can go in a CV. We will consider what is the minimum information and what are the advantages and disadvantages of giving more details. Then you will write the personal section of your CV.

Time needed for this unit: 1 to 2 hours

Note: there is no need for a heading to the section, but you can call it "Personal" or "Personal details" or "Personal information" if you like.

THE MINIMUM INFORMATION

The minimum personal information in a CV is:
- name
- address
- date of birth

NAMES

Here are some examples of names adapted for use in the UK:

```
I.V. (Bala) BALACHANDRAN
K.I. SUKHLAL ('Suki')
GHEBREGIORGIS Estefanos (Stefanos)
Olufemi (Olu) OSINUBI
Ruksana BEGUM
TRAN Tu Manne, Tu Manne TRAN, Tu-Manne TRAN or Tumanne TRAN
Pilar GARCIA Lopez, Pilar GARCIA-LOPEZ or Pilar GARCIA
R.K. PAU (known as Jimmy)
```

Notice that they all show their family name with CAPITALS (underlining will do just as well), and some of them include the nickname used by their English colleagues and friends. It's not essential to adapt your name or to use a nickname, but you can prevent a lot of problems with ignorant British people if you do this. You might think it's important to include a nickname if your referees know you only by this name.

DATE OF BIRTH

You must have an exact date of birth to operate effectively in the UK. If the official date is wrong, for example because your parents protected you from military service, write your real date of birth. You can explain any differences from the dates on official documents when you are offered a job.

OTHER PERSONAL INFORMATION

Most people give more than minimum personal information. Here are other usual headings: Telephone, Place of Birth, Nationality, National Insurance Number, Gender or Sex, Marital Status, Children, Childcare arrangements, Health. These headings require only a few words after them.

Read the following notes about the headings before you decide if you should use them.

TELEPHONE

This is very important. Please include a number, even if it belongs to a friend. To show that it's not your number, you can put "Contact telephone". Make sure that anyone answering that phone knows that you are using it for job applications. If they have limited English, make sure you have arranged that they can take a message so you can phone back the caller.

If you are worried about speaking English on the phone, you should practise with friends. You could ask a friend to take a message even when you are at home. They may even be able to arrange the interview for you. It is, however, increasingly common for employers to interview informally on the phone. Try to avoid this if it worries you, and request a face-to-face interview.

AGE

It's a good idea to include your age to save the employer some mental arithmetic.

PLACE OF BIRTH, NATIONALITY, NATIONAL INSURANCE NUMBER

There are two approaches to these items. One approach is to put your place of birth, nationality, refugee status and National Insurance number to show the employer that you are a genuine refugee with the right to work. After all, you have a foreign name and background and the employer will wonder why. The other approach is to put only your N.I. number and perhaps "work permit not required" to show that you are not trying to work illegally.

Approach 1 (example)

```
Mr Witold GIERCZ
Date of birth: 31.6.60
Place of birth: Szeczin, Poland
Nationality: Polish
Residence status: Refugee with 'exceptional leave to remain in UK' –
with right to work and probably settle after 5 years residence (date of
arrival in UK: 9th June 1986)
Work permit not required.
N.I. Number: AV 13 46 78 E
```

Approach 2 (example)

```
Mr Witold GIERCZ
Date of Birth: 31.6.60
N.I. Number: AV 13 46 78 E
```

You have to decide which approach to use. Employers may be less prejudiced against refugees than they are against most foreigners, as refugees are sometimes considered to be more deserving than other immigrants. So it may be helpful to mention your refugee status, as long as you make it clear that you have the right to work and are not likely to return to your country soon.

GENDER/SEX, MARITAL STATUS, CHILDREN, CHILDCARE

Under the headings of Gender or Sex, Marital status, Children, Childcare arrangements, two approaches are again possible. They affect your job chances differently depending on whether you are a man or woman.

Women

If you are a woman, it's usual to put your gender and all the other information: marital status, number of children, childcare arrangements.

Many women prefer not to put any of this information, because employers may be prejudiced against employing married women and women with dependent children. However good your childcare arrangements, or however long you have been married without children, employers will assume you will take time off to look after sick children or have babies. So they might prefer a man.

On the other hand, many employers believe that women often make better workers than men. These employers may be less prejudiced against married women and women with children. You will also ease their worries if you can show you have made childcare arrangements. You may be able to put something like "Full-time childminder with mother-in-law back-up," for example.

You have to choose which approach is right for you. If you don't include marital status, you are behaving as a normal man would. If you include the fact that you are married and have children, this should make no legal difference to your chances of a job. Unfortunately it often does make a difference. But if the information is not on your CV, employers will probably ask you at interview if you are married and have children. It is not legal to ask you this if they would not ask a man the same question, but it does happen. If you feel that you have been treated unfairly because you are a woman, you could go to your local CAB (Citizen's Advice Bureau).

Men

If you are a man, it's quite normal to leave out all the above headings. There are sometimes advantages to including marital status. It depends on the job. Some employers think that married men are more steady and reliable, for example. If your name is not obviously masculine, include "Sex: Male" in your CV.

Men and Women

Don't mention other members of your family, unless they are involved in childcare or they are your own children. In the UK the "nuclear family" – wife, husband and children – is the only kind of family recognised for most purposes.

HEALTH

Put "Health: good" if possible. If you have had long periods of illness in the past, you should mention them in the "Other information" section(s) to explain otherwise suspicious gaps in your career. In this case you can put "Health: good (see below)". Or you may prefer to wait until the employer asks.

REVIEW OF HEADINGS

To summarise, you must include name, address and date of birth. It is polite to include your age. You should, if at all possible, include a telephone number. You must show that you can work legally in the UK, but it's up to you whether you want to give more details of your status. If you are a man, there is no need to give any information about wife or children, but employers often approve of married men. If you are a woman, employers will generally want to know if you are married and if you have children.

Your main competitors are usually men who may feel no need to give more than the minimum information. On the next page are two examples. Have a look at these. Are they right or wrong to omit other details? How do you feel about the way these CVs handled personal details? Your answer to this question should help you to decide how to handle them in your CV.

Now think about the details you want to put in *your* CV. Tick the items on the following list which you would like to include in the personal section of your CV. This unit has given you some guidelines to help you decide what is right for you.

TASK 12

FAMILY
grandfather's name, mother's name, your name, your wife's name, your children' names and ages
NAMES AND CONTACT
your surname, your personal name, your religious name, your nickname, your initials, your home address, a telephone number
STATUS
your date of birth, your age, your place of birth, your nationality, your ethnic group, your languages, your residence conditions, your police registration number, your National Insurance number, your sex, your marital status
HEALTH
your doctor's name, your recent serious diseases, your periods in hospital, any drugs taken

CURRICULUM VITAE

Shler Karim
104 Oak Tree Park
LONDON SW17
01 627 7891

Date of Birth: 10th October 1951

EDUCATION AND QUALIFICATIONS

1964 - 70	Secondary and High School Suleymania Secondary School Certificate 10 subjects High School Certificate in Arts subject
1971 - 74	University of Suleymania B.A. in Economics
1983 - 84	Chamber of Commerce Advanced Business English course, London.
1984 - 85	Postgraduate Diploma in Business Administration Glasgow Polytechnic. - Accountancy, Personnel, Marketing, Statistics. - Economics.

CAREER HISTORY

1974 - 80	Assistant finance officer for export company in Baghdad. Responsible for monitoring international monetary system e.g. currency exchange rates etc. preparing reports and analyses for the management committee; implementing the financial policy of the company.
1981 - 83	Lecturer in Economics. University of Baghdad
1985 - 86	Bonjuk Housing Association - London Housing Aid Worker. Duties include translating; interviewing potential families; organisation of assessment system; liaising wit local council housing department.

Referees: 1. Dr Alietin Siait   2. Mrs Barbara Watson
               37 Cross Street   44 Arlington Road
               Hemel Hempstead   LONDON SW17
               Herts
               Lecturer in Psychology   Teacher of Business Studies
                                            (Chamber of Commerce)

CURRICULUM VITAE

Name:	Scott Ashley NAYLOR		
Address:	34 Pike Street, Handsworth, Birmingham BM10 43W		
Tel. No.	(0981) 307062 – Home	(0981) 234937 – Work	
Age:	31	Date of Birth: 29 August 1950	

Married with two children: boy (8) girl (1)

EDUCATION

Fairlawn Comprehensive School, Bristol	Sept. 1961 –	July 1966
Brindley Technical College, Bristol	Sept. 1968 –	June 1970
Lanchester Polytechnic (part-time)	Nov. 1970 –	July 1972

QUALIFICATIONS

*C.S.E.	Maths, English, Physics, Technical Drawing Woodwork, Geography	1966
*G.C.E. 'O' Level	Technical Drawing	1966
H.M.C.	Mechanical Engineering	1970

EXPERIENCE

Technician Apprentice	Sealco Ltd.	Coventry	1970 – 1974
Junior Welding Engineer	Sealco Ltd.	Wolverhampton	1974 – 1975
Welding Engineer	Worldwide Engineering Services Ltd.	London	1975 – 1979
Welding Superintendent	Minichip Modules Ltd.	Birmingham	1979 – 1981

Experienced in engineering work planning, troubleshooting, quality control, commissioning of new plant including EBW and friction welding, as well as argon arc and electric and gas welding. Recent direct experience of man management.

OTHER ACTIVITIES

Pianist with local jazz group.
Plays regular club football.

REFEREES

Mr B.J. Cameron	Mr James McKenchnie	Mr John Patel
Personnel Manager	Welding Engineer	Company Director
Minichip Modules Ltd.	Sealco Ltd.	38 Pike Street
6-9 Brigstock Road	14 Hyecroft Street	Handsworth
Birmingham BM3 9QZ	Coventry CY6 1DS	Birmingham BM10 4EW

You have now done all the preparation for writing the personal section of your CV, choosing all the relevant headings.

Now complete the "Personal" section of your CV. Be as brief as possible and use the two examples of CVs for reference.

MAIN TASK A

unit 4

education

Time needed for this unit: 4 hours

You have made a good start on your CV with the personal section. The next section is more complex because your choices need to be based on many more factors.

The basic items for this section are:
- dates of attendance for education and training
- names and locations of schools etc.
- names of courses where relevant
- qualifications achieved.

In this unit you will learn which elements to put in this section and which to put in the "Other information" section(s). You will learn how to gain recognition for your qualifications and how to compare your educational background with the British system. You will consider the problem of overseas qualifications being undervalued. You will learn about the status of various English language qualifications. Finally you will learn how to describe any gaps in your education caused by political or financial problems. Then you will write the "Education" section of your CV.

EDUCATION AND TRAINING

The "Education" section should include all your general education from the age of about eleven, and your relevant professional training, including English language training. The section should not include part-time classes for leisure interests.

It is sometimes important to mention different items under "Education" depending on the job you apply for. Look at how this is done in the following examples.

Example 1
Rhoda Douglas's Personal Information Chart for a job as a SENIOR TYPIST:

Education

Parkhill Comprehensive, Darlington (2 'O' Levels in English and French, CSE Grade 3 Maths, Needlework, Music) 1978-84
Parkhill College (RSA Stage 3 Typewriting, RSA Stage 1 Book-keeping, Business Communications, and Audiotyping) 1984-5
Office Supervisor Employment Training (NE Electricity) 1988

Other Information

Canoeing gold medal, North of England Colts Champion 1984
Public Service Vehicle Driving Licence 1986
Car maintenance evening class 1986-7

Example 2
Rhoda Douglas's PIC for a job as a COACH DRIVER:

Education

Parkhill Comprehensive, Darlington (2 'O' Levels in English and French, CSE Grade 3 Maths, Needlework, Music) 1978-84
Parkhill College (Office studies course) 1984-5
Darlington Bus Company PSV Driver's Course (Merit pass) 1986
Car maintenance evening classes, Darlington Adult Education Centre, 1986-7

Other information

Canoeing gold medal, North of England Colts Champion 1984
Office Supervisor Employment Training (NE Electricity) 1988

You can see how Rhoda Douglas emphasised her office training for the senior typist job and her bus driver training for the coach driving job.

Another kind of training that you should think about is language training. If English is not your first language, you should include any English language training in your home country or the UK.

Example

1978-83 University of Krakow, MSc Mechanical Engineering (minor subject: Technical English)
1985-6 Vauxhall College, London, RSA English as a Second Language Profile Certificate.

This example shows that the writer has good technical English for his job and also everyday British English from his course in the UK.

Before you choose the important educational items to put in your own CV, you can practise with the following task. This involves choosing the right educational background to go with a particular job.

TASK 13

Look at this list of courses and qualifications. Tick the ones you would include under "Education" for a job as a Production Manager for a Paper Factory. Then check with the Answers section at the end of this unit.

1. Certificate in forestry
2. Canoeing certificate
3. 5 "O" Levels (W. African Board)
4. Ghanaian Army Officer Training
5. BTEC Diploma, Business Studies
6. English Literature evening class
7. Model making evening class
8. Carpentry & Joinery TOPS Course
9. Origami (paper folding) evening class

There is often confusion between the terms "Education" and "Training". This might help:

Education educates you for life.
Training trains you for one job.

If you want to show that your training is particularly good, you could divide your "Education" section in two and put "Training" in a separate section.

MATCHING YOUR QUALIFICATIONS WITH BRITISH ONES

Equivalence = matching the value of qualifications from different countries.

It is obviously important for employers to know how your qualifications compare with British ones. This matching of different qualifications is known as **equivalence**. There is no official equivalence of overseas qualifications to British ones, but The National Academic Recognition Information Centre (NARIC) gives advice which many employers and educational institutions follow. For professions like architect, accountant, civil engineer, lawyer etc., there are professional associations in the UK who will offer recognition to some overseas qualifications. For teachers, the Government's Department of Education and Science Qualifications Branch can give "qualified teachers" status, to those with appropriate qualifications.

The best first step is to apply to NARIC with your qualifications.

If an individual wishes to obtain *general advice* on the standard of an overseas qualification in British terms and the recognition that is likely to be accorded to it he/she may contact NARIC. NARIC does not assess courses, institutions or qualifications, but provides advice on the standard of academic qualifications at any level, obtained in any country overseas. The information is based on its experience of the attitudes of British institutions to such qualifications in the past. If this is not available, factual information on a particular foreign institution or qualification will be offered. Institutions requesting advice are free to accept or reject it as they wish. Enquirers should send full details of a person's previous education with copies of all relevant certificates and transcripts of marks with translations as necessary. NARIC does not offer personal interviews to individuals wanting advice on their qualification, nor does it provide "To Whom It May Concern" letters. However, an explanatory letter from NARIC may be useful for individuals, particularly to show to prospective employers.

To apply to NARIC you also need a professionally made translation of any non-English certificates and marks.

Apply to NARIC for equivalence. You can get a form from them by ringing 01-930 8466. Their address is NARIC, The British Council, 10 Spring Gardens, London SW1A 2BN.

TASK 14

Whatever NARIC says about your qualifications, you will be able to explain them to employers much better if you can compare the education, qualifications and training that you received with general British equivalents. There is a NARIC book which covers the educational systems of 142 countries. It includes equivalence to UK qualifications and it's available from libraries (or for sale at £50!). If you can't find it at your local library, ask if they can borrow it for you from another library. The title is *International Guide to Qualifications in Education* (formerly "A Guide to Overseas Qualifications"), Mansell Publishing Ltd, 6 All Saints St, London N1 9RL, ISBN 0 720 11716 X, 1987.

Here are some examples of equivalents:

SSC, Pakistan (equivalent to 5 'O' Levels/GCSEs)
            (or 'O' Level/GCSE standard)
Baccalaureat, France (equivalent to 3 'A' Levels)
            (or 'A' Level standard)

TASK 15

From the NARIC book or any other sources you can find, fill in the tables below to compare your country's education and training with the system in England, Wales and N. Ireland. (Scotland has a different system).

EDUCATION AND TRAINING

_____	= PRIMARY SCHOOL
_____	= SECONDARY SCHOOL
_____	= FURTHER EDUCATION (COLLEGE)
_____	= HIGHER EDUCATION (UNIVERSITY)
_____	= TRAINING

QUALIFICATIONS

_____	= "O" LEVELS (TO 1987) GCSE (FROM 1988)
_____	= "A" LEVELS
_____	= HIGHER NATIONAL DIPLOMA
_____	= FIRST DEGREE (BA/BSc)
_____	= SECOND DEGREE (MA/MSc)
_____	= DOCTORATE (D.Phil/Ph.D)

PROFESSIONAL TRAINING

What qualifications do teachers need in your country?

_____ = P.G.C.E. (TEACHING)

What qualifications do accountants need?

_____ = A.C.A. (ACCOUNTANCY)

What qualifications does your profession need?

_____ = (YOUR PROFESSION)

ATTITUDES TO OVERSEAS QUALIFICATIONS

If you look through the International Guide, or talk to refugees from other countries, you may feel that the British consistently undervalue overseas qualifications, particularly from developing countries. Don't make this point to employers, but consult an educational adviser. The best would be WUS (World University Service), Compton Terrace, London N1, Tel. 01-226 6747. If you cannot easily contact WUS, ask libraries or advice centres about local sources of educational advice. Find out from them if the situation has improved at all recently. For example, overseas teachers may soon gain better recognition.

LANGUAGE COMPETENCE

Your competence in your own language and any others should go in the "Other information" section(s) unless it is needed for your job, as English is of course.

How do you demonstrate your competence in English?

English language qualifications are not as useful as you might think. Employers are generally much more impressed by your command of English in your CV, form-filling, letters, phone calls and interview than by paper qualifications.

For professional and managerial jobs, English language "O" Level, CSE or GCSE are the only commonly recognised qualifications, though Cambridge Proficiency or similar level EFL exams might be appreciated by some employers.

For other "white-collar" (office, technician, supervisor) jobs, "Communication" certificates may be useful. The RSA, CGLI, LCCI and BTEC are examining boards which may have Communication exams at your local college.

For any other kind of job, any English language qualification may be useful, but your performance in person is more important. In any case certificates taken by native speakers of English (AEB Basic English, for example), are more widely known than EFL or ESL certificates.

TASK 16

Put the English qualifications below in order of prestige among employers. Check with the Answers section at the end of the unit.
1 Cambridge Proficiency EFL
2 Cambridge First EFL
3 GCSE/"O" Level English
4 AEB Basic English
5 RSA Business Communication
6 RSA ESL Profile
   Note that the examinations and examining bodies mentioned here are known to

educationalists and many employers by the initials, and the full names are rarely used. For your reference these are:

CSE – Certificate of Secondary Education
GCSE – General Certificate of Secondary Education
"O" Level – Ordinary Level General Certificate of Education
"A" Level – Advanced Level General Certificate of Education
EFL – English as a Foreign Language (for people overseas)
ESL – English as a Second Language (for UK residents)
RSA – Royal Society of Arts, Manufacturing and Commerce Examining Board
CGLI – City and Guilds of London Institute Examining Board
LCCI – London Chamber of Commerce and Industry Examining Board
BTEC – Business and Technician Education Council Examining Board
AEB – Associated Examining Board
Cambridge – University of Cambridge Examination Syndicate

GAPS IN YOUR EDUCATION

Do not include failed examinations in your CV. If you attended a course but didn't receive the qualification, mention the course briefly to explain what you were doing.

You should account for all the years of your adult life in your CV, however briefly. Interruptions for political or financial reasons need to be explained briefly. You may have to give more details at the interview.

EXPLAINING ANY GAP IN YOUR EDUCATION CAUSED BY POLITICAL OR FINANCIAL REASONS

Education interrupted by civil war
Education halted due to military service
Education terminated owing to family's financial needs
Relocated to area without educational establishments
Expelled from university for political activity against government

You should now have a good idea of how you can best present your education and training. You know which items to include under "Education", mentioning equivalence where possible. You know to include English language training but not to rely on its qualifications. You know about unfair attitudes to equivalence and you know how to challenge them without ruining your job chances. You also know the importance of explaining any gaps in your education.

See Unit 5, page 50, and Unit 6, page 57, for more about explaining gaps in your career.

Write the "Education" section of your CV as you would present it for the job that you would prefer to do.

Look at this CV for an example of a British graduate's education, and look back at the others for reference too.

MAIN TASK B

Name:	BRENDA HOPKINS	**Address:**	5 Blank Street Brighton
Date of Birth:	12.2.62		East Sussex BN1 6AB
Nationality	British	**Tel:**	0273 606881

EDUCATION

1974 - 78	Houndshill Comprehensive School, Ealing 9 'O' levels: English Language, English Literature, History, Economics, Geography, French, Maths, Chemistry. Biology.
1978 - 80	Garston Park Sixth Form College, Northants 3 'A' levels: Chemistry (A), Maths (B), French (B)
1981 - 84	University of Sussex BSc Chemistry with Economics minor (Class 2.1) Courses followed include Organometallic Chemistry; Organic and Applied Inorganic Chemistry; Molecular Enzymology; Medicinal Chemistry; Computer Programming. Economics minor: Industrial Relations, Science and Policy; The Analysis of Industrial Problems. Final Year project "...................."

WORK EXPERIENCE

August 1980 - March 1981	Junior lab technician with Brownstone Pharmaceuticals, working in their Quality Control Laboratory: routine testing and analysis.
March 1981 - September 1981	Spent two months travelling in France, staying with friends in Paris and Toulouse before going to Israel to work on a Kibbutz.
1982 (Summer vacation)	Courier with American Leadership Study Group.
1983 (Summer vacation)	Junior lab technician with Brownstone Pharmaceuticals.

INTERESTS & ACTIVITIES

At my Sixth Form College, I helped to organise the school community action group: we arranged visits to old people in the area and organised a Christmas Party for residents in a local old people's home.

I have taken part in several student drama productions at university and in my second year was Treasurer of Sussex University Dramatic Society.

Other interests include badminton, squash, films (I am a member of the campus Film Society) and community work. Through "Link-up", the student community action group, I have helped to run playgroups on local estates and organised weekend outings for old people.

Other Skills:	Good spoken and written French Driving: have held a full licence for two years Computing: some knowledge of BASIC and FORTRAN.
Referees:	Dr Anthony Smith School of Chemistry and Molecular Sciences University of Sussex Falmer, Brighton D S Freeman, Personnel Manager Brownstone Pharmaceuiticals High Marsden Industrial Eastate High Marsden Northants

ANSWERS

TASK 13   1, 3, 4, 5, 8

TASK 16   3, 1, 5, 4, 2, 6

employment

unit 5

You are well on your way to completing your CV. Now you have to write the section which is usually most important. It is where you show how your past employment will suit you for the job you want now.

In this unit you will learn how to describe past jobs and to review and rewrite descriptions. You will learn how much detail to include. We also suggest how to explain gaps due to childcare and household management, unemployment, failed business ventures and political/military activity. You will learn what jobs to leave out or mention very briefly. You will also learn about *accreditation* courses which can help you to prove your skills to employers. Finally you will write the employment section of your CV.

Time needed for this unit: 4 hours

DESCRIBING YOUR PAST JOBS

The basic items needed here are:
- dates of employment
- job titles
- descriptions of jobs where relevant
- employers' names and locations.

You must try to attract employers' attention to the work you have done which is most like the work you are applying for. Jobs which are irrelevant can be mentioned briefly, without a description. If there are many of them you can just put the general dates and something like "various clerical posts" or "sales and administration work for various firms".

Jobs which are relevant need to be emphasised. If you go for a job as a football coach, your CV should say more than "Football coach 1982–6, Somali National Team". You could put more details like "Coached team to semi-finals of East African Cup on three occasions. Trained three players for World Cup teams".

If you can briefly describe past jobs and make them sound like the jobs you are applying for, you are half way to an interview. Employers are happiest employing someone who has done similar work before.

As you are a refugee or migrant in the UK, any work you have done in the UK is relevant. This can include Community Programme work or Employment Training, such as work experience placement or other state-funded schemes with the former MSC or Training Agency. The type of work you did may be very unlike what you wish to apply for now, but the fact that it is in the UK gives it an extra value.

It's not necessary to include past salary or reasons for leaving past jobs, though you should be ready to give this information at interview.

If you had management or supervisory jobs you should mention how many staff were under you.

Example

Financial Controller, Kseniya Textile Enterprise.
Managed accounts department with staff of 15.

or

Supervisor, injection moulding section of Chung-Ta toy factory. 7 operatives, 2 fitters, 1 cleaner.

It's very important to explain clearly what you did in your past jobs, as this is the main factor which an employer will judge you on. It can be difficult, particularly as many overseas jobs have no British equivalents. This makes things extra hard, as you must try to explain unfamiliar concepts in a very few words.

CVs can be up to two pages long, but employers often have no time to read a second page. One page CVs are more effective if you can choose only relevant material.

So, your descriptions of past jobs need to be very short, perhaps 5, 10 or 20 words maximum, depending on what other details must be there. You should make enough space to give longer descriptions for a job which is very like the one you are applying for. This may be a different job in different job applications.

Here are examples of 5, 10 and 20 word descriptions of jobs that probably do not exist in Britain:

Noodlemaker

Hand-making noodles for restaurants/shops. (5 words)
Prepared noodles with special craftsman's technique and sold them. (10 words)
Using demanding traditional methods (e.g. spinning noodle dough), prepared noodles of various types and sold to local and national outlets. (20 words)

Dramaturg

Artistic director and script editor. (5 words)
Supervised quality of theatrical productions, vetted and edited play scripts. (10 words)
Employed by theatre to maintain high artistic standards of scripts and productions. Advised writers, directors, actors, funding committees and officials. (20 words)

These descriptions show the noodlemaker's and dramaturg's jobs in a brief and confident style. The descriptions explain to British employers the basic features of jobs that the employers know nothing about.

NOODLEMAKER'S SKILLS

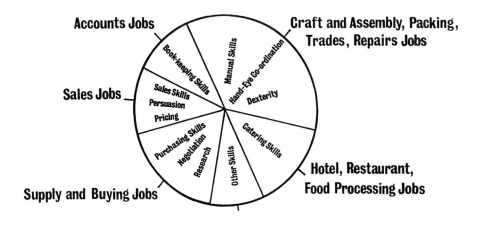

It is not enough, though, to describe your job accurately. You must also describe it in such a way that the employer sees how it connects with the job you apply for.

A noodlemaker, for example, could have skills for a job in a restaurant, a job as a salesperson, a job involving accounts, a job involving negotiated purchases, or a job involving quick fingers and concentration. It is then necessary to change the job description to show how the noodlemaker's work is similar to these jobs.

Here are some possible descriptions of the noodlemaker's work in CVs used for various different kinds of job:

Sales job

Noodlemaker – sold noodles to restaurants, shops and individuals in many challenging sales contexts.

Accounts job

Noodlemaker – ran own business keeping double-entry accounts for equipment, stock, individual customers, credit and cash sales, capital and loans.

Restaurant job

Noodlemaker – involved in retail and service catering, food preparation, customer contact, hygiene and stock control.

Job for quick fingers (e.g. electronic component assembly)

Noodlemaker – rapid production of up to ten thousand units per day involving exact hand-eye co-ordination.

You can show that your experience can fit a variety of jobs. But *you* must show the employer that your skills from your old job are transferable – that they can be just as useful in the new job. The employer will not make these connections for you.

Now think of your own preferred job and practise describing your past jobs so that they fit the job.

TASK 17 Describe your own past jobs in 5, 10 and 20 words, so that your descriptions will be ready for your CV.

REVIEW YOUR JOB DESCRIPTIONS

Whenever you write something important, you should always review it and improve it. It's often best to leave it for a day or two before coming back to look at it again. It's surprising how much you can improve things that way.

It's even more important to show your job descriptions to other people – your doctor, your health visitor, your child's teacher, or anyone who has a professional job and knows you. There is more about using other people's expertise in Unit 9 on *Getting help and support*. It's amazing how much other people can help your writing by looking at it from a different point of view.

Look at these descriptions of past jobs. What's wrong with them? Check with the Answers section.

TASK 18

1 Production manager, Redisil Furniture Factory, 1981-85
  Managed production of furniture in factory.

2 'Garnje steng' administrator, Department of Economic Affairs, 1981-1985
  I was responsible for maintaining efficient procedures regarding 'garnje' in the Department, in conjunction with the 'garnje taran' manager.

3 Trade Union Official, Confederation of Labour, 1981-85.
  Agitated against cruel fascist dictatorship. Organised three dangerous strikes and 10 go-slows in various industries, then thrown into prison on trumped-up charge.

Return to your 5, 10 and 20 word descriptions of past jobs a day or two after writing them. Review them and rewrite them if necessary.

TASK 19

TECHNICAL TRANSLATIONS

As mentioned before, translations are often necessary, particularly to describe technical terms. These terms are important to show that you really are a professional. The best thing to do is to find someone who does the same job in this country, and discuss the current terms used.

For basic business terms, there are bilingual dictionaries in 11 community languages available from National Extension College. Or you may find the *"English Duden"* of assistance. This is a vast pictorial dictionary of technical processes with 25,000 objects illustrated. See the list of books at the back of the book.

Otherwise try reading professional journals and magazines, textbooks and reference books. You will find these in your library. The librarian will be happy to help you. You can also ask for help from professional associations, Chambers of Commerce and Jobclubs. If you still have difficulties, a commercial translation agency may have access to technical translators in your field.

TASK 20 Choose a few important technical terms from your profession(s) which you would have to explain to a British employer in your CV. Try and find their exact technical translations.

EMPLOYERS ADDRESSES

It isn't necessary to give full addresses of past employers, unless they are referees – see Unit 7. In this case give the full address in the referees section and put "address – see referees below" next to the employer's name. You should put the name of the city and the country. You can give full details later if it is required. At that stage, the names of individual people who you worked for (contact names) may well be needed.

Any jobs you have had in the UK, even temporary, manual or casual jobs, should be made easy for employers to check. You can put a contact name and phone number or the full address if there is enough space.

TASK 21 List all your past jobs with full addresses, contact names and telephone numbers. Use this list to choose relevant details for each job application.

GAPS

As with gaps in education, gaps in your employment record must be explained or employers may assume you were unemployed or in prison for crime rather than political reasons. Use the suggestions in Unit 4, page 42, to explain political or financial problems where these are appropriate. Other reasons for gaps may be:
- health – explain these in "Other information" section(s) – see Unit 6, page 57.
- childcare and household management (as parent or wife)

- unemployment (perhaps due to your political stance)
- failed business ventures.

Women with an important family role often mention this on their CVs when they apply for jobs. This explains the gap in their paid career by emphasising the skills they used as housewives and mothers. This example of a CV comes from the popular women's magazine "Family Circle". The applicant is using this CV to apply for a responsible office job. For this reason she stresses the budgetting and organisational skills of household management. Other jobs that you apply for might require different emphasis. Any experience of this kind should relate clearly to your proposed new job.

CURRICULUM VITAE

Name: MARIAN BURWOOD
Address: 33 Anywhere Road, Anytown, Anyshire KD3 7UB
Date of birth: May 19, 1951
Available for work: Immediately

Work experience:

1977 to the present - Full-time household manager.
I left my last job as a personal secretary two months before the birth of my eldest son. I have spent the past ten years at home raising my three children and managing the household budget and some of my husband's business accounts. This has been a rewarding experience, but now that my youngest child is at school, I am eager to return to full-time work. The past ten years have taught me how to cope with many different demands, and how to organise my time more efficiently. Although I have been away from the office environment for some time, I feel that I can return to it with more maturity.

1974 to 1977 - Personal Assistant to Mr Benson, Benson Building Works.
Duties included confidential correspondence, organising Mr Benson's diary and arranging overseas business trips. I also supervised the work of a general secretary and an office junior.

1972 to 1974 – Secretary, Benson Building Works.
Day-to-day secretarial duties included correspondence, shorthand and typing, filing, logging invoices and expenses, supervising office junior.

1969 to 1972 – Clerical Assistant, Thomson Publishing. General clerical duties included typing manuscripts and letters, sorting post, filing, ordering office supplies, answering phones.

1967 to 1969 – Receptionist, Ingram's Surgical Supplies. Duties included operating the main switchboard, receiving visitors, sorting post, some typing.

Education:
1962 to 1967 - Orpington Secondary School
4 'O' Levels in English, Maths, Geography and Cookery.

1967 to 1968 – Nightclasses in shorthand and typing
RSA Certificate Stage II.

Childcare: I have arranged for a local registered childminder to look after my children before and after school. My mother will look after them during school holidays.

Interests: I am a member of the Red Cross and do voluntary work at a local hospital. I play squash and enjoy cooking.

The important thing about this CV is that it shows a gap in employment positively. It shows how job-related skills are being developed and maintained without paid employment. Voluntary work can be presented in the same positive way as household management. You should always be able to find examples of relevant activities at any period of your adult life. In the next task, you can see how a positive approach makes a gap in employment into a useful piece of experience.

TASK 22

Look at these descriptions of gaps in people's **employment record**. There are four different people. Person A was a prisoner. Person B ran a succession of businesses while officially unemployed. Person C was a housewife. Person D was a freedom fighter. They describe their past in four or five different ways. Identify which descriptions belong to the same person. Then decide which is the best description for each one to choose for their CV if they apply for a general management position. Check your ideas with the Answers section at the end of the unit.

Employment record = your past jobs, and the start and finish dates of each.

1. In prison
2. Unemployed
3. At home
4. Barred from appropriate work by government order, tried to sell jeans from a stall, then T-shirts, then scarves. Then had tea trolley but tea urn broke. Started river ferry business, forced out by competitors' cartel.
5. Wrongly imprisoned as a traitor despite proving my innocence time and time again. (My lawyer was working for the government).
6. Fighting for National Liberation Movement
7. Political prisoner
8. Guerrilla
9. Childcare and household management for family (2 children)
10. Looked after my two little boys and my husband
11. Launched several small businesses (retail, catering, transport) while barred from normal work by regime
12. After mass round-up of political opponents, the government detained me without trial for five years
13. Military service with secessionist forces. Drove trucks, trained recruits, organised supplies
14. I took up arms against the oppressive regime that killed my uncle

and cousins. After five years' struggle, my superiors authorised by
return to civilian life.

15 While in detention for anti-government writings, organised sports,
welfare and food distribution, made models and toys for sale abroad.

Try to explain any gaps in your own record in a similar positive way to items 9, 11, 13 and 15. Items 1, 2, 3, 7 and 8 are too short. Items 4, 5, 10, 12 and 14 are too detailed and emotional.

COURSES TO SHOW EMPLOYERS YOUR SKILLS

There are several **"accreditation"**, "portfolio" or "prior learning" courses at colleges in Britain. These titles refer to a new type of college course which is mainly aimed at women returning to work after raising children but is useful for anyone without a full employment record in the UK. Accreditation courses can help you to build up a portfolio, showing examples of your skills and experience. These may be in the form of writings, photographs and other material. This portfolio can then be shown to employers when you cannot show your worth through referees or conventional career history. If you had to leave your country suddenly without documents, these courses could be of particular help to you in proving your skills to employers.

Accreditation = showing the value of what a person has learned with a certificate or some other form of official recognition.

Find a local accreditation course and decide whether it could be useful. If not, think about taking other courses to build your skills up while you apply for jobs.

TASK 23

You have now practised describing jobs and reviewing your descriptions. You have looked for technical translations and decided what addresses and contact names are relevant. You have considered what level of detail about past jobs is needed for new applications. You have decided how to explain any gaps in your career and investigated accreditation and other courses. Now you are ready to write the employment section of your CV.

Write the "Employment" section of your CV. Remember that in Task 11 in Unit 2 you decided whether or not you would use **reverse chronological** order.

MAIN TASK C

ANSWERS

TASK 18 1. The description only gives information already in the job title. More details of the number of staff and types of production process are needed.

2. This gives no translation of "garnje", "steng" or "taran", making it impossible to understand. Exact translations are often difficult, but an attempt is necessary – for example "Garnje steng" (production quotas and budgets); "garnje" (production quotas); "garnje taran" (budget control).

3. This is too emotional and political. A better version would be: "Organised trade union action in disputes in various sectors, maintaining confidence of workforce, until consequent illegal detention by totalitarian regime."

Whatever you write, you should try to imagine what a particular employer will think of you when they read your description.

TASK 22 Repeat scattered descriptions and annotate each one with Person A or B, etc.
Person A: 15 best.

Person B: 11 best.

Person C: 9 best.

Person D: 13 best.

other information

unit 6

You have now done the main parts of your CV, but you can add special appeal to it with a few more details. In this unit we look at the headings you can use and those you shouldn't use. We also match suitable information with various job types.

Time needed for this unit: 2 hours

POSSIBLE HEADINGS

"Other information etc." is NOT a suitable heading, though "Other information" is possible if no more exact heading will suit. The best headings list skills and achievements, not just interests. You should certainly not use the heading "hobbies", which sounds childish. Look at these two examples:

Example 1

Interests
Computing (BASIC programming & wordprocessing)
Conjuring (perform tricks at children's parties)

Other information
Lay preacher in Baptist church, 1983 – present

Example 2

Skills and Achievements

Qualified swimming instructor/lifeguard, 1969
Member of City Council, Hue, 1971-1973

Languages

Fluent Vietnamese and English
Good French

Example 2 is better, as the headings show more what the person can do, not just the things the person likes doing.

Here is a range of common headings:

Personal achievements
Posts of responsibility
Special skills
Skills and abilities
Childcare
Extra-curricular activities
Activities and interests
Languages
Professional Associations
Publications and research
Interests
Skills and achievements
Other activities
Other/additional information

One or two of these headings should be right for your CV. Here is a selection of items that could be included under some of these headings:

1. Qualified herbalist
2. President of chess club
3. Good spoken Pushtu, spoken and written Dari/Farsi
4. Mountaineering, typing, French
5. Clean driver's licence
6. Arc welding, spot welding and rivetting
7. I have raised 6 children since 1974, alone since husband's detention in 1979
8. Member of Kurdish Association Committee and Haringey basketball team

Extra-curricular = not part of official studies or work.

9. "Cryogenic properties of molybdenum", University of Santiago Press, 1972. Investigation into high-altitude molybdenum applications, (unpublished research), University of Santiago 1971–3.
10. Decathlon gold medal, regional games 1979
11. First Aider's Certificate 1982
12. Writer/translator of "Measles inoculation", booklet for local Community Health Council 1984
13. Car maintenance evening classes 1985–7

To prepare for your own choice of items and headings, try Task 24.

TASK 24

Choose one item from the above list for each of the headings given. For example, you could choose Number 3 to go under the Languages heading. Then check with the Answers section.

EXPLAINING GAPS

The "Other information" section(s) are also useful for explaining gaps in your career. If you put the explanation here it doesn't get in the way of your impressive academic or professional record. The best heading for these explanations would be "Other (or Additional) Information".

Here are two examples:

> Registered disabled no B1100/229. I usually use a wheelchair but can walk short distances.
>
> Nursed sick mother through terminal illness 1985-1988.

Unless you are asked specifically, do NOT show employers information such as the following three examples, at least until you are offered a job:

> Hospital treatment for hepatitis 1965 and 1974-5. Condition in remission ever since.
>
> Nervous breakdown 1982-3 following war trauma and marriage breakdown. No problems since this time.
>
> Imprisoned Sept 1987-Jan 1988 for dangerous driving. Licence to be reinstated next year.

Remember that your CV should show the best side of you. You don't need to offer information that shows you in a bad light.

We have now looked at a number of headings for the "Other information" sections of your CV. We have also considered what information you should and should not include. Now it's nearly time for you to decide the heading(s) for your own CV. Two should be enough for this section. But remember that for different jobs, you will choose different items. Do one more task on this theme before deciding your own approach.

CHOOSING THE RIGHT ITEMS

You should only include two or three items under each heading, so you have to choose them carefully. They should either relate directly to the job, or show that you are generally an interesting and successful person.

To prepare for choosing the right items for your CV, do Task 25.

TASK 25

Look again at the list of items on page 56. Choose two or three items which would suit the following jobs. You can check the answers at the end of the unit.
- (a) Afghan Centre Administrator
- (b) Community Health Council Secretary
- (c) Travelling sales representative
- (d) Service engineer (washing machines)

You can place your language competence on this scale:
(starting from the best)
<u>Bilingual</u> in Cantonese (Chinese) and English
<u>Fluent</u> Amharic
<u>Good</u> Portuguese and Italian
<u>Conversational</u> French
<u>Basic</u> Arabic

Bilingual normally means speaking two languages very well indeed. Among linguistic minority groups and English as a Second Language teachers, it may also mean "regularly speaks more than one language".

We have looked at the possible headings for this section now. You have thought about what items to choose and how to describe them. Select those headings now and decide on the items to describe.

MAIN TASK D

Write the "Other information" section(s) of your CV.

ANSWERS

Here is a complete list of the items and their possible headings **TASK 24**

Personal achievements 1, 2, 3, 7, 8, 10, 11
Posts of responsibility 2, 8
Special skills 1, 2, 3, 4, 5, 6, 11, 12
Skills and abilities 1, 3, 5, 6, 11, 12
Childcare 7
Extra-curricular activities 1, 2, 4, 8, 10, 11, 12
Activities and interests 1, 2, 3, 4, 6, 8, 10, 11, 12
Languages 3
Professional Associations (none)
Publications and research 9
Interests 1, 2, 3, 4, 6, 8, 10, 11, 12
Skills and achievements 1, 2, 3, 4, 5, 6, 7, 8, 10, 11, 12
Other activities 1, 2, 3, 4, 7, 8, 10, 11, 12
Other/additional information (all)
Of course you were only asked to choose one item for each heading.

(a) 3, 5 & any other **TASK 25**
(b) 11, 1, & any other
(c) 5, 10, 12 and 4 or any other
(d) 5, 12 & any others

unit 7

referees

Time needed for this unit: 2 hours

In this unit we will consider the question of *referees*. We look at the various kinds of referee, how to choose a referee, how to ask someone to be a referee and what you expect of them.

KINDS OF REFEREE

Referees write **references** about you and send them to employers.

A football fan would say that there are only two kinds of referee – unfair, and very unfair. A job applicant may need three kinds:
- your present or past employer (the most recent, usually)
- your present or past college (usually the most recent)
- a respectable person who knows you.

These three kinds are often called:
- a professional referee
- an educational or academic referee
- a personal referee.

Many people use only two referees.

If you are over 25, or if you have recently had a job, include a professional referee. These referees are by far the best unless you have just left full-time education. In this case, you should include an academic referee. The other kind of referee is a personal referee. Many employers like a personal reference because it shows you as a person rather than just as a student or an employee.

So it is best to be ready with three referees in case an employer wants three, or in case you need an academic referee for one kind of job and a professional referee for another.

60

PROFESSIONAL REFEREES – EMPLOYERS

Your present employer or your most recent employer is the usual professional referee. If you use a less recent employer, you may have to explain why. A good reason could be that your more recent job was only a temporary manual job to do while you looked for something more suitable.

You should always give the name, the job title, the address and the telephone number of your professional referee. The name should normally be of the person who is or was your immediate superior (your manager), or of the Personnel Manager or Personnel Officer. Ask your colleagues or ex-colleagues who is the best referee before you leave the job, or afterwards if necessary.

ACADEMIC REFEREES

It's best to choose a teacher or lecturer who knows you well. Then the reference will be based on actual knowledge of your studies. If you can't find a teacher to do this, you can ask the Head of Department to give a reference. In the summer holidays, this is usually the only possibility unless you know your teacher very well.

PERSONAL REFEREES

These are the hardest to choose. By tradition, personal referees have usually been your doctor, your priest or your bank manager. But these people may hardly know you. So try to think of someone who knows you, and who has a regular, respectable, responsible job or other good status (such as chair of a voluntary organisation). The main thing is to make sure that they will write you a good reference! It's quite possible that they will show you what they write, or plan it with you beforehand. You can't use a relative because they would be considered to be too biased. You can often, for example, ask a friendly ex-teacher to be this kind of referee.

To help you think about the problems of choosing a referee, try Task 26.

TASK 26

Look at this list of people. Which would you choose to be your professional, your academic, and your personal referees? Choose one of each, assuming they will all write equally good references. Check with the Answers section.

1. A doctor you met once
2. A priest/religious leader you talk to every week
3. An unemployed teacher
4. A relative
5. A teacher from 10 years ago
6. A current teacher at your college class
7. The Head of Department of your college
8. Your employer in your own country
9. The solicitor who helped you get refugee status in the UK
10. The secretary or other official of your community group
11. Your next-door neighbour, a plumber
12. Your child's childminder
13. The employer who gave you two weeks' work last year
14. The employer from your government training scheme.

Now think about the people that you know. Who will you choose?

ASKING PERMISSION

It is very important to ask a referee's permission before you give their name to a possible employer. It makes the referee feel better about you. The other reason to ask permission is that you can explain about the job you are going for. If possible, give the referee a copy of the advert or the job description. That helps the referee to write a more appropriate reference.

If you are in work at present you may prefer not to ask your employer for a reference. You may not want them to know you are "looking around". In this case, it is acceptable to put below your list of referees: "Please contact me before taking up references."

Make sure that you have the correct name for your referee, the correct title (Ms, Mrs, Dr, Mr, Miss), job title, address and phone number. Many references are now given on the phone.

You can also phone to ask permission. Do this if your referee has given you references before and you just want to give new details about a new job possibility.

Otherwise it is more polite to write a letter asking someone to be a referee. The letter also helps the referee to remember details about you that they might have forgotten. It is useful, too, to be able to give your referee written details of the job you want, so that the reference can mention relevant facts.

Now practice writing a letter to ask for permission.

Fill in the gaps in this letter.

TASK 27

Dear

You may _____ that I was a member of the _____ Community Group committee last year. I am _____ to say that we have _____ funding for another year. I know that your _____ work helped to make this happen.

Now I am _____ for a job as a _____ I would be very grateful if I could _____ your name as a referee.

If this is _____, please telephone me or leave a message at this number: _____.

Thank you.

Yours _____

We have now looked at choosing referees, and asking permission. Let's consider what kind of things a reference should say.

THE REFERENCE ITSELF

Professional and academic referees will usually say that you are punctual, hard-working, and good at your course or your job. They may say that you have a good personality, are honest, get on well with people, and are helpful. There will be varying important qualities depending on the job you apply for, and they should write suitable references each time. Personal referees will not mention punctuality, hard work or job or course skills, but they may mention the other qualities above. There is usually one slightly negative statement to make the rest seem more credible. Future employers do not usually take references very seriously, unless the reference is surprisingly negative. So choose your referees carefully to avoid this.

You should now be able to choose good professional, academic and personal referees. You know how to ask their permission and you have a good idea of what they will say about you. This means you can complete the last part of your CV.

MAIN TASK E

Choose three referees (professional, academic, and personal) and ask their permission to quote their names. Then write the "Referees" section of your CV.

ANSWERS

TASK 26
1. No
2. Yes, Personal, especially if you are applying for a welfare job
3. No
4. No
5. No
6. Yes, Academic
7. Yes, Academic, if your teacher is on holiday
8. Probably not, because of the danger of delay
9. Yes, Personal
10. Yes, Personal
11. Maybe, personal
12. Probably not
13. Yes, Professional, if no other professional reference
14. Yes, Professional, if no important paid job.

TASK 27 Here is one suggestion. Other answers are possible.

Dear Mr Smith

You may *remember/recall* that I was a member of the Community Group committee last year. I am *glad/pleased/happy* to say that we have *secured/raised/been guaranteed/been awarded* funding for another year. Your *hard/professional/expert/untiring* work helped to make this happen.

Now I am *applying/looking* for a job as a sales representative I would be very grateful if I could *mention/quote/give/use* your name as a referee.

If this is *agreeable to you/possible/acceptable*, please telephone me or leave a message at this number: *01-222 4466*

Thank you.

Yours sincerely

YOUR FINISHED CV

3

UNIT 8
Page design

UNIT 9
Getting help and support

UNIT 8 PAGE DESIGN

Headings and sub-headings.

TASK 28 **Choose style of headings and sub headings**

Handwritten or typed text.

Columns.

TASK 29 **Choosing column style**

Translations.

Using capitals, underlines, brackets etc. to show translated terms.

TASK 30 **How to present a translation**

Layout.

TASK 31 **Choose overall page layout**

MAIN TASK F **(= A + B + C + D + E) – Assemble parts of CV into whole and produce a good layout**

UNIT 9 GETTING HELP AND SUPPORT

What now?

"Getting a job" and self-help groups.

Why involve other people. Importance of trying ideas on friends, research and mutual support.

Source of information.

TASK 32 **List sources of information**

Sources of support.

TASK 33 **List sources of support**

In Part 3 we will develop your CV writing skills in relation to the whole document. We will also work on getting help to make it better.

page design

unit 8

You have now completed all the individual sections of your CV. It's time to think about packaging the whole CV as a coherent, impressive document. You need to use the techniques of a publisher's editor and designer to do a good job.

Time needed for this unit: 1 hour

HEADINGS AND SUB-HEADINGS

You need to decide how to present your main heading "CURRICULUM VITAE", your section headings ("Education", "Employment" etc.), and perhaps sub-headings ("Dates, Job title and description", "Employer", "Training", "Qualifications" etc.)

You can use any of the styles in the following list, which goes from main heading down to sub-headings:

- CAPITAL LETTERS UNDERLINED
- CAPITAL LETTERS
- Capital and Small Letters Underlined
- Capital and Small Letters

When you use capital and small letters, make sure that you put capital initial letters on all important words in a heading or sub-heading.

Example

CURRICULUM VITAE

Mrs Tu Tram PHAN, 119 Collingwood House, N. Peckham Estate, London SE17 1AL Telephone: 01-222 2222

PERSONAL DETAILS

Date of Birth: 23rd Oct 1946

National Insurance Number: YB 12 34 56 M

67

TASK 28 Choose the style of headings and sub-headings (if needed) for your CV.

HANDWRITTEN OR TYPED TEXT

Any CV should have perfect writing or typing: no crossings-out, no Tipp-Ex, no ink spots. If you have to use Tipp-Ex, you may find that it is not visible on a photocopy; but you should avoid using photocopies unless you are sending CVs to many employers at once. For any job you really want, don't use a photocopy. If your CV is typed, write a short letter of application by hand. Some employers think your handwriting tells them a lot about you – which is tough if you use a different alphabet in your first language. If your handwriting in English is very good, or you can't find a typewriter, a hand-written CV is acceptable. Lined paper can be used *under* the paper to trace horizontal lines.

COLUMNS

It is usually neater to write details of your education and employment in two or three columns.

Example:

1976-78	Secondary School, Hanoi, Vietnam	School-leaving Certificate
1983-85	Part-time Advice Worker (Housing, Health Services, Education, Employment)	Refugee Action (address: see Referees below)

However you can present the information without columns, too.

Example:

Secondary School, Hanoi (School-leaving Cert.) 1976-1978
Part-time Advice Worker (Housing, Health Services, Education, Employment) for Refugee Action 1983-1985 (address: see Referees below)

Columns normally look better, especially for dates.

Think about how you're going to set out the information. Decide whether to use columns, how many, where, and how wide.

TASK 29

TRANSLATIONS

If you want to include both the name or word for something in your language and an English equivalent, it is sometimes difficult to present them clearly. Here are some examples of ways to do it.

Examples:

Docent (University Lecturer), Zagreb
'Docent' (= University Lecturer), Zagreb
Docent/University Lecturer, Zagreb
DOCENT, University Lecturer, Zagreb
Docent, University Lecturer, Zagreb
Docent arapskog knjizevostna, filosofski fakultet, univerzitet Zagreba,
Lecturer in Arabic Literature, Faculty of Humanities, Zagreb University

In most cases the English equivalent is sufficient on its own.
If your language has accents like ˜ ˆ ´ ` which are difficult to find on English typewriters, write them in neatly by hand, or leave them out if the word is understandable anyway.

Decide how to present any translations in your CV.

TASK 30

LAYOUT

British culture and Western culture generally are more and more concerned with the visual appearance of information. How something looks is often thought to be as important as what it says. "Designer" and "style" are current buzz-words – fashionable concepts which affect employers' attitudes just like everyone else's. Visual Awareness (mainly graphic design) is a part of the syllabus for most British Business Studies courses and many other courses in schools and colleges.

So it's very important to give a pleasing visual impression with your CV, in the details mentioned above and in the general appearance.

TASK 31

Look at the page-shapes below, which represent different ways of laying out the words of a CV on a page. Which one looks best? Could you lay out your own CV like this? If not, should you change your CV to make the visual appearance better? Check with my suggestions at the end of the unit.

In this unit you have thought about headings, columns, handwriting and typing, translations and general layout. You now have all the elements you need to make a good CV, except for feedback from other people. It can be vitality important to involve others in your job search. That is the focus of the next unit.

MAIN TASK F

It's time to set out all the parts of your CV together on one or two pages, and see how it all looks.

In Main Tasks A, B, C, D and E you wrote these sections of the CV:
- Personal
- Education
- Employment
- Other information
- References

Combine all your sections to make a CV for your preferred type of job. Look at it from the page design point of view, and adjust it to look as impressive as possible.

Think about what changes you would make for a different kind of job. Produce a second version of your CV with these changes on.

ANSWERS

TASK 31

1 is best, because there is plenty of white space for margins, the headings are neatly aligned to the left, and the writing is in pleasing rectangular blocks. Try to produce a similar impression with your CV.

unit 6
getting help and support

**Time needed for this unit:
At home – 1 hour. Out – 4 hours**

You have done two versions of your Curriculum Vitae for two different kinds of job. That's a great achievement, and you may now be ready to send CVs to employers. This could be in response to job advertisements, or in the hope that there might be a suitable vacancy with an employer who has not advertised.

There is much more to learn about looking for a job. You could try using the companion course to *Writing a CV*, which is called *Getting a Job*. It's available where you got this course.

The purpose of the present course is to make sure that you have the basic tools for writing good CVs and supporting statements (which can be in the form of an application letter). The most important thing you need now is a person or, better still, people to advise you on making your CV as good as possible.

WHY INVOLVE OTHER PEOPLE?

You need people to look at your CVs and supporting statements (see Unit 10) because you need someone to look at them objectively, in the way an employer will look at them. You may be too close to the subject to see a mistake or a wrong impression. **Other people's ideas can improve the items you include, the way you describe them, and the overall presentation of your CV. They can make the difference between getting and not getting a job.**

WHO CAN HELP

In your daily life you may meet people who know more than you about getting jobs in the UK: people who have been educated in this country, people with a wide range of contacts, or people who know the kind of employment you are interested in.

Examples of such people could be your child's teacher, your health visitor, social worker, doctor, librarian, bank or building society manager. Or they could be neighbours, members of voluntary organisations and community groups, or even if you are lucky a professional Careers Officer or Careers Adviser. If you think hard about who you know there is probably at least one person who could give good advice about your CV.

HOW TO ASK

The key to getting people's help is showing them that you will not be causing much trouble. Ask someone if they have a few minutes to spare, and explain that you will not be asking for anything difficult or complicated. All they have to do is look at the CV you wrote. Then they can take as much or as little time as they like to read it, comment on it, suggest improvements or suggest places you can go to for more help. Don't tell someone you don't know very well how important their help is to you as they will probably get embarrassed. Treat the situation casually, and then they will not worry that you will be a problem for them. Show that you do not want or expect very much help, but a little help would be valuable. That way your helper can feel free to choose to give more help without feeling under pressure.

SOURCES OF INFORMATION

One of the most important things about involving other people is to share information – for example, which items in a CV might be most useful and which employers have vacancies. How can you find out about useful vacancies and useful approaches to a CV?

You can go to the library for daily newspapers, magazines and journals, textbooks, factual background and reference books. The local business and employment scene will be known by advisers at the Jobcentre, the Careers Office, local Council officers stimulating local employment, Chambers of Commerce and Trades Councils. If you have a particular profession, their professional association(s) will be able to advise you too. Note that many professions have more than one association.

Make a list of useful sources of information for your job needs.

TASK 32

SOURCES OF SUPPORT

Your friends and family will offer you support and the sources above will give you information. You will also need the support of well-placed individuals and agencies to provide specific help, not just general information. They may also, if you are lucky, help with practical things like typing, photocopying, postage and telephone calls. These people are actively committed to helping others. Some are responsible for particular groups: refugees, jobhunters, people in a particular area, or people from a particular country. Their help can be very valuable. You can find them in refugee agencies, colleges and adult education centres, advice centres, community groups, voluntary organisations and sometimes Jobcentres, careers offices, or social services departments.

TASK 33 Make a list of useful sources of support for your job needs.

That is the end of this unit. You have thought about the energy and expertise that other people could bring to your jobhunting efforts. Don't neglect these because you are too humble or too proud to involve other people. You may help them as they help you. Everybody deserves help, and everybody needs it.

SUPPORTING STATEMENTS

UNIT 10
Supporting statements

4

UNIT 10 SUPPORTING STATEMENTS

Why write a supporting statement. Supporting statements as signs of understanding job, good arguing skills, writing skills. Brenda Hopkins application letter.

How to write a supporting statement. Using job specifications to structure a supporting statement. Matching items from CV with job specifications. Selection and ordering of best items.

TASK 34 **Underline relevant items to telephonist job***

TASK 35 **Order importance of matched items***

Explaining each important item. Add extra facts to items and make suitable sentences for numbered supporting statement.

TASK 36 **Make numbered supporting statement for telephonist job***

Polishing your statement. If job requires high writing skills, organising supporting statement – focus, elaborate, conclude. Numbered form acceptable otherwise.

TASK 37 **Write a "Focus" and "Conclusion"**

Polishing your statement. Need to get friend or self-help group's advice on drafting supporting statement.

TASK 38 **Shorten overlong supporting statement***

Summary

MAIN TASK G **Write supporting statement for an advertised job**

* = example answer given

supporting statements

unit 10

A supporting statement is often required by employers in professional jobs. The *supporting statement* is a written explanation of how the experience and skills that you have listed in your CV (or application form) can be applied to the job you are applying for. The statement can be part of an application form, or an employer may ask you to attach it to a CV.

If the employer doesn't ask for a supporting statement, you should still send a short letter with your CV. It serves to highlight the most important aspects of your background. This kind of *application letter* is a kind of supporting statement, though a short one. If, on the other hand, the employer asks applicants "to apply in writing, stating why they feel they are suitable for this post", this can be a longer piece of writing.

This unit takes you through the reasons for writing supporting statements. Then it goes through the planning stages, matching a job's requirements with your skills, making notes and completing a statement.

WHY WRITE A SUPPORTING STATEMENT?

When you have spent such a long time on your CV, it may seem unnecessary to start again writing a supporting statement, too. **But many jobs require such statements, and it's a good idea to point out what makes you particularly suitable for the job.** Your application letter needs to be rather more informative than: "Dear Sir or Madam, I am writing in the hope that you may have a suitable vacancy for me. I enclose a Curriculum Vitae. Thank You. Yours faithfully".

Such a letter fails to include anything about you which would make anyone want to read your CV.

The idea of a supporting statement is that it shows how well you can argue that you

Time needed for this unit: 4 hours

Supporting statement = a written explanation of how the experience and skills that you have listed in your CV can be applied to the job you are applying for.

Application letter = 1. a short letter which has a supporting statement in it. The letter accompanies your CV. *or*
2. a long letter which has the information of a CV and a supporting statement in it.

really are a suitable applicant. Two aspects are important – your arguing skills or ability to persuade, and secondly the actual facts that you choose to emphasise. The first shows that you have a good personality and communicate well. The second shows how ready you are for the requirements of the job. Both these aspects are very important. If you have identified the right items from your background, but the employer comments that your writing is "a bit woolly", or "long-winded", you lose credibility. On the other hand it doesn't matter how well you argue if you don't fit the employer's requirements.

Here is an example of a supporting statement in the form of an application letter, from the person with managerial experience described in Unit 4 page 43.

```
Mr J Smith                                              5 Blank Street
Bloggs & Co.                                            Brighton
Winton                                                  East Sussex
WN2 3ZB                                                 BN1 6AB

                                                        2.11.83

Dear Mr Smith,

        I enclose my application for the vacancy of Management Trainee as advertised in the Guardian on
1.11.83. I am interested in this post as I believe that my Chemistry degree with Economics minor will
give me a useful broader base for technical management. I also enjoyed my vacation work experience with
Brownstone Pharmaceuticals where I saw the importance of good management/employee relations.

        I would prefer to attend for interview during the Christmas vacation (Dec 12th - Jan 6th) with the
exception of Dec 20th - 27th, but other times could be arranged if necessary. I would be free to take
up an appointment after graduation from August 30th 1984.

Yours sincerely, etc.
```

This letter picks out the key points of the applicant's background which make her suitable for this particular job. It would be very useful in getting her an interview.

HOW TO WRITE A SUPPORTING STATEMENT

The initial planning of a supporting statement involves making a list of the job's requirements, and then matching your skills and experience to these requirements.

Example

Job as administrator
advertised as needing
– experience of
   public service
– management experience
– organisational ability
– communication skills

Your CV includes
– 10 years government service in
   home country
– organised staff of 20 in bank
– represent refugee group in
   discussions with Home Office,
   council and other funding bodies

KING'S COLLEGE HOSPITAL

Tel: 274 6222 (extension numbers are given in the text)

SENIOR TELEPHONIST

Required to join our switchboard team. In addition to general telephonist duties the post will involve the day to day supervision of staff. You will also be expected to participate in an 'on call' rota out of hours and at weekends.

You should have good interpersonal and supervisory skills, and have had experience of the PABX system and preferably be GPO trained. Previous hospital experience would also be an advantage.

Hours: 40 per week.

Wage: £104.87 per week inc. plus 15% bonus.

Application forms and job descriptions available from: the Unit Personnel Department, Tel: Ext. 2408/2752, quoting Ref. No. A/5433.

Read the above job advertisement and **specification** for a senior telephonist. Below is the career history of a person applying for the job. Underline items in her CV which match the qualities required in the advertisement. Then check with the Answers section.

Jeena Muortat

Employment

1986 - now	Night Telephonist (PABX system), Visnews Ltd
1985 - 86	Childcare (daughter born 1985)
1982 - 85	Supervisor, Darkroom, Visnews Ltd
1981 - 82	Part-time Receptionist/Telephonist, Visnews Ltd
1978 - 81	Darkroom Assistant, Camerashy Photographs Ltd
1976 - 78	Auxiliary Nurse, King's College Hospital

Number the items you underlined in order of importance, then list them in that order. Check these with the Answers section.

TASK 34

Job specification = description of what is involved in a particular job. Usually sent to applicants before they fill in an application form. More detailed than a job advertisement.

Person specification = description of what skills, qualities and experience are expected of someone to do a job successfully. Often used in equal opportunities jobs and many others (see Unit 2, page 18).

TASK 35

EXPLAIN EACH IMPORTANT ITEM

If you have to write a supporting statement, follow the same procedure as you did just now – underline and then order the items in your CV which match the job requirements.

After that, you have to explain how each item matches the job.

Examples:

My experience as a _____ makes me suitable for this post.

As I have 10 years _____ I feel I would be appropriate for this post.

My _____ skills are applicable to this job.

My _____ skills fit the job requirements.

My experience in _____ matches the requirement for _____ of this position.

This needs some practice. You will probably need to think of various different ways to say "because", and various different ways to say "suitable".

Here's some practice in making the link between experience and job requirements. Plan Jeena Muortat's supporting statement for the senior telephonist position. In fact such a position may not require a supporting statement, or indeed a CV, if the company supplies an application form.

But the same process of selection and highlighting, matching, ordering and explaining links should be used in the application form and in the interview itself. The advantage of using this kind of job as an example is that the requirements are straightforward.

TASK 36

Look at these extra facts from Jeena's CV. Use them with the four items already underlined and ordered, to write four sentences in support of her application. Check with the Answers section.

1. Working in busy newsfilm agency. Night staff of 15. Many international calls.

2. Supervised staff of 5, night and day shifts. Enjoyed responsibility.

3. 3 years experience with this system.

4. Familiar with hospital routines and organisations.

POLISH YOUR STATEMENT

Many jobs may require a well-written statement in good English, organised into one or more paragraphs. Others may not require perfect English and allow a statement in note form. For a job where good English writing could be very important, here is some guidance on how you could do this.

It is best to follow a pattern like this:

1. FOCUS – One sentence explaining which job you are applying for.

2. ELABORATE – One sentence for each point (there are four in Jeena's application).

3. CONCLUDE – One sentence explaining that you think your statement shows you are suitable and should be considered.

Write a Focus and Conclusion sentence for Jeena's supporting statement.

TASK 37

FOCUS – ELABORATE – CONCLUDE is a form of "discourse organisation", as linguists would say. There are other forms, for example elaborating first and focussing later, which are also common, but this method is preferable. Many British people imagine that foreigners don't "come to the point" (focus) and don't show when they have finished (conclude). This method will help you to avoid these criticisms.

Be very careful of your English when you write a supporting statement. It's much harder to get this right than a CV. Get native English speakers to advise you.

This supporting statement is too long as an application for the same telephonist post. Remove repetition and irrelevant material and rework it to make it an effective supporting statement. Check your version against mine in the Answers section.

TASK 38

With reference to the vacancy for the post of senior telephonist currently being advertised as a vacancy due to the retirement of Mrs D. Knight, whom I know quite well as my duties involve talking to her every day, I should like to apply to fill this vacancy myself. I should like to draw your attention to the following points which I have made as comments under the numbered headings below in order to indicate to you my suitability for this post, for which I believe I am very well qualified both by experience and training.

1. My hospital career so far has entirely been with this hospital, so I am well-acquainted with hospital life in the NHS hospital system, which would be relevant for this job because it is within this hospital.

2. My telephonist skills and abilities have been demonstrated time and time again during the three years I have spent at King's College Hospital as a Junior Hospital Telephonist, working at all hours and with all kinds of staff, sometimes under pressure because of emergencies, as when I had to track down Dr Forbes who was urgently needed in theatre and I tried no less than fourteen different extensions as his radiopager ('bleeper') was not working. Luckily I saved the day and the operation was a success.

3. My training was excellent at the Holborn telephone exchange and I learned how to connect calls, how to deal with enquiries, all the tricks of the trade so to speak, working for the GPO or British Telecom as it is now.

4. I have had plenty of experience of PABX systems (6 weeks in 1983 when the regular operator was ill) and know all about the switching systems and queuing, conference phone facilities and monitoring calls.

All this experience and training makes me very suitable indeed for promotion to senior telephonist, in fact if I am not considered I will probably look for another job, so I very much hope that you will be good enough to at least offer me an interview for the above position as senior telephonist to work with the King's College Hospital switchboard team in a more senior capacity. I would also like the chance to be a supervisor sometimes as it would make a change.

SUMMARY

When you are planning a supporting statement, first get all the information you can about the job. (This may require some research on your part if you are applying for a job that has not been advertised.) You may be able to get hold of a job specification. Otherwise you will have to work from the job advertisement. Then follow this method:
- Match points from your life with points from this information.
- Put these points in order of importance.
- Add any details to expand the points.
- Make one sentence explaining why each point matches the requirements of the job.
- Number the points OR combine them in one paragraph (or more) using the FOCUS – ELABORATE – CONCLUDE method.
- Review and edit your statement with expert advice.

In this unit you planned a supporting statement for Jeena Muortat, and edited another for the same job. You are now ready to write a supporting statement for a job that you want.

MAIN TASK G

Obtain a job advertisement, and if possible job specification, for a job which interests you. Review your CV and make sure it fits the job. Then write a supporting statement for it, using the method outlined above.

ANSWERS

1986 – now	Night Telephonist (PABX system), Visnews Ltd	**TASK 34**
1985 – 86	Childcare (daughter born 1985)	
1982 – 85	Supervisor, Darkroom, Visnews Ltd	
1981 – 82	Part-time Receptionist/Telephonist, Visnews Ltd	
1978 – 81	Darkroom Assistant, Camerashy Photographs Ltd	
1976 – 78	Auxiliary Nurse, King's College Hospital	

1. Telephonist (twice) **TASK 35**
2. Supervisor
3. PABX system
4. King's College Hospital

Here are four possible sentences. Yours may be different. **TASK 36**

> 1. I am experienced in general telephonist duties as I am a telephonist for a busy newsfilm agency with a night staff of 15, handling many international calls.
>
> 2. I am suitable for supervisory work because I supervised a staff of 5, on night and day shifts, and enjoyed the responsibility.
>
> 3. I know the PABX system well, having had three years experience with this system.
>
> 4. I would expect to work well with the switchboard team as I am familiar with hospital routines and organisation.

Numbered points are acceptable as a style of supporting statement for many jobs, though a continuous paragraph is more common.

This is one way that Jeena's supporting statement could be composed. (Note – the headings "focus – elaborate – conclude" are to show you how the statement is organised. They should NOT be included in your application). **TASK 37**

FOCUS

> The following points support my application for the post of senior telephonist.

ANSWERS continued

ELABORATE

I am experienced in general telephonist duties as I am a telephonist for a busy newsfilm agency with a night staff of 15, handling many international calls. I am suitable for supervisory work because I supervised a staff of 5, on night and day shifts, and enjoyed the responsibility. I know the PABX system well having had three years experience with this system. I would expect to work well with the switchboard team as I am familiar with hospital routines and organisation.

CONCLUDE

I therefore hope that you can consider my application seriously as I believe that I would be very effective in this post.

TASK 38 Here is a suggested rewording.

With reference to the post of senior telephonist, I should like to apply to fill this vacancy, and draw your attention to the following points.

1. I have three years experience as Junior Telephonist within King's College Hospital, so I am familiar with general telephonist duties and hospital procedures.

2. I have some experience of the PABX system, and have operated all its main features.

3. I am GPO trained.

I hope that these points will allow you to consider my application. I am also very interested in the post's supervisory aspects.

PRESENTATION EXTRAS

UNIT 11
Additional documents

UNIT 12
Professional presentation

UNIT 11 ADDITIONAL DOCUMENTS

Testimonials. Where appropriate.

Certificates. Usual practice.

Translations. Attested or notarised and other translations.

Photocopies and originals. When to use which.

TASK 39 **Choose when to show testimonial, reference, attested or notarised translations, certificate, CV, supporting statement***

* = example answer given

UNIT 12 PROFESSIONAL PRESENTATION

Typing, word-processing and desk-top publishing.

Paper quality.

Employment consultants.

TASK 40 **List useful services**

Photographs.

Final words.

SOME USEFUL BOOKS

additional documents

unit 11

This unit tells you NOT to send additional documents with your CV and application letter. Employers do not want to see certificates, *testimonials* and translations until they offer you a job (if ever).

These documents are valuable, however, and we shall look briefly at how they are used in Britain.

Time needed for this unit: 30 minutes

TESTIMONIALS

A testimonial is like a reference, but employers generally dislike testimonials and like references. The reason is that a testimonial is an OPEN reference given to you by a past employer. A reference is a CONFIDENTIAL document which the referee is not supposed to show you. So references are supposed to be more truthful than testimonials. In practice, though, good references are often given by current employers when they want someone to leave them! It is also quite common for friendly referees to give you a copy of the reference they wrote about you.

A testimonial may also be called an "open letter" and it may begin with the words "To whom it may concern". It is generally very positive, but so are references.

Don't send testimonials with job applications. If you think a testimonial is particularly useful, perhaps because it was written by an expert in your field or gives particular details about your work, then you can put "Testimonial available" at the end of your description of the job.

Testimonial = a letter praising your work and given to you at the end of a period of employment by the employer.

Example

1968-78 Export and Technical Manager, Rubber Seals and Sealants Company. Contributed to 200% volume increase in exports over ten years and 300% sales increase. Testimonial available.

87

CERTIFICATES

Evidence of all your qualifications (school certificates, degree certificates, diplomas, training certificates, English language qualifications etc.) should be available for employers to see at or soon after interview. Only show them at interview if asked. Have translations available then, even if they are unofficial translations. Never send certificates before an interview.

If you couldn't bring your certificates with you when you left your country, and cannot get them sent to you now, it will now be difficult for you to have the qualifications assessed by NARIC (see Unit 3, p. 38). But you may well not need to show certificates to obtain a job.

Research has indicated that in Sri Lanka, 75% of success in job applications is due to qualifications and only 25% to performance at interview. This is partly because of a system which insists on interviews for every applicant. In the UK very few applicants are interviewed. Success in British job applications is probably in the opposite ratio to the Sri Lankan one – perhaps 75% interview and 25% qualifications. So qualifications are not all-important, and if for any reason you cannot produce evidence of your qualifications, you may be accepted anyway. It is possible that you will be asked to state or swear to a notary, or commissioner for oaths (a kind of lawyer) that you really have the qualifications.

ATTESTED OR NOTARISED TRANSLATIONS

Attested or **notarised translation** = a translation which the translator has sworn or promised to be accurate in the presence of a lawyer. This means the translator can be prosecuted in court if the translation is not accurate.

Notaries also **attest** or **notarise translations** of your certificates and other official documents. Some translation agencies are part of legal offices and you can have translations made and attested in the same place. Such translations are not often required, but they may be if your qualifications are vital for your new job. It's often enough to have an unofficial translation of your certificates until someone asks you for a notarised one. But it will save time and perhaps embarrassment to have a notarised translation of any important qualification ready with you at interview.

PHOTOCOPIES AND ORIGINALS

In general, never let other people have your original documents. Always send photocopies unless they insist on originals. Most refugees know how frustrating it is when you need a document but the Home Office keeps it for a year or more. Fortunately few other organisations insist on seeing original documents; in fact, some prefer to have photocopies in case they lose the originals.

TASK 39

Look at this list of documents and then answer the questions about them below. Check your answers with mine at the end of the unit.

references
testimonials
certificates
attested/notarised translations
CVs
supporting statements

1. Which of the documents are sent to employers before interview?
2. Which of the documents should be taken to interview?
3. Which of the documents are seen by employers if they offer you a job?
4. Which of the documents are disliked by employers?

That is the end of this unit. You have nearly finished the course. The last unit is the one for the extra touches to make your CV and supporting statement as good as they can possibly be.

ANSWERS

TASK 39

1. CVs, supporting statements
2. All except references (unless you have a confidential copy)
3. All
4. Testimonials

unit 12
professional presentation

Time needed for this unit: 30 minutes

In this last unit we add some final, more or less expensive suggestions which you may be able to use if you have some money or some good contacts. They are not necessary to a good CV, but they may create an absolutely professional impression which tilts the balance in your favour.

TYPING, WORD PROCESSING (WP) AND DESK-TOP PUBLISHING (DTP)

Your CV should look fine if it is typed on a manual typewriter, but it will look even better if you use:
- an electric typewriter
- a word processor
- desk-top publishing

Employers rarely see manual typing these days, so if you can use an electric typewriter it will look more professional. If no-one you know has one, it may be worth hiring one or using a typing service. See under "Secretarial and Office Services" in the Yellow Pages for typewriter hire and typing bureaux.

Modern typing bureaux use word processing, which means that they can do **bold** or *italic* letters as well as normal roman letters. This is very useful with CVs. All your headings and sub-headings can be in **bold**, and any words in your language which you translate can be in *italic*.

If you can find a word processor yourself, make sure that the computer has a good printer. If it prints only 'draft quality' or 'near letter quality' using a 9 pin dot-matrix printer, an electric typewriter may be more useful. You can always take a computer disc to a word processing or printing service and ask for them to print out your CV with a good printer (daisywheel, inkjet or laserprinter, or possibly 24 pin dot matrix). But if you have to choose between a cheap printer and a word processing or printing service, as CVs are quite short, it may be cheaper to ask a word processing service to type and print your CV.

Desk-Top Publishing is a form of computer software that can take word-processed typing and change the size and shape of letters, and include graphic symbols and illustrations. There is no reason to use DTP for a CV. A DTP package might be useful if you have a good visual design sense, perhaps for making a box all around the margins, or slightly larger lettering for the words "Curriculum Vitae", but that is about all. Beware of "overdoing" the design. Some employers might question an applicant's sense of priorities. A CV is, after all, a piece of information, not a work of art.

PAPER QUALITY

A much easier way to make your CV look top quality is to use top quality paper, like the paper of this page. It really makes an enormous difference to the impression your CV gives. Buy thick paper from a commercial stationer's or office supplies service.

EMPLOYMENT CONSULTANTS

Employment consultants supply, at a *high* price, a range of services from counselling and psychological testing to writing CVs for you. If you just want them to write a CV, it can still be quite expensive as they will need to interview you and to understand the details of your background. You can look for these agencies in the Yellow Pages under "Employment Agencies" or in the employment advertisement pages of quality newspapers.

The advantage of using a consultant to write your CV is that they know the British job market, and may supply up-to-date advice that you can't get elsewhere. A disadvantage is that everybody using the service finishes with similar-looking CVs, so employers can easily recognise them and know that they are not all your own work.

Employment consultants = people paid by jobhunters to help them find jobs.

Make a list of people you know with electric typewriters or word processors, and look in the Yellow Pages for typing and word processing bureaux and employment consultants. Telephone a few of them and ask their prices, in case you ever need them.

TASK 40

PHOTOGRAPHS

Some employers like to see a photograph with a CV. A look at your face will give them an idea whether you are pleasant to look at and friendly in appearance. This could be quite important in jobs dealing with the public or any job involving sales or customer/client contact. If your age is against you, but you look young, your photograph could be reassuring to the employer. Be sure to dress smartly for your photograph, as you would for an interview, and look pleasant. There's no need for an enormous smile, but don't look gloomy.

Get a good quality passport-sized photograph, preferably in colour, and attach it to the CV. A holiday snap will not be good enough. Try a photo booth in a shop or station, or ask a professional photographer.

FINAL WORDS

The aim of this book has been to develop your skills so that you can write a new CV every time you need one. I have tried to avoid giving one model for you to copy, so that you can choose from a range of examples and make up your mind for yourself. You have considered why certain approaches work better than others in composing your CV and supporting statement. This makes you able to write a CV which is right for you, in a way that is better than any adviser can write it for you. You should now have the ability to review and change your own writing as necessary.

I hope the course has been useful. If you have any comments, please send them to the Training Unit, British Refugee Council, 240–250 Ferndale Road, London SW9 8BB.

some useful books

Bilingual Dictionaries of Business Terms, Suzanne Looms, National Extension College, 18 Brooklands Avenue, Cambridge CB2 2HN
The Business of Communicating, Nicki Stanton, Pan 1982
Communication for Business Students, C. J. Parsons, Arnold
English Duden, Oxford University Press
Handbook for Business Writers, Doris H. Whalen, Harcourt Brace Jovanovich
Help Yourself to English, Robert Leach, Elizabeth Knight, John Johnson, National Extension College (see address above)
International Guide to Qualifications in Education, Mansell Publishing Ltd. Available from libraries
The New Unemployment Handbook, Guy Dauncey, National Extension College (see address above)
Principles and Techniques of Effective Business Communication, I. A. Krey, V. Metzler, Harcourt Brace Jovanovich
Sussex University Careers Service Teacher Advice Pack
Workseekers, ILEA Learning Resources Branch